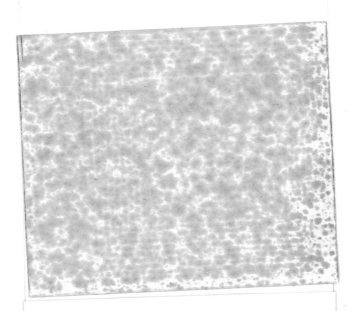

Caregiving of Older Adults

Choices and Challenges:
An Older Adult Reference Series
Elizabeth Vierck, Series Editor

Caregiving of Older Adults,
Louise Fradkin and Angela Heath

Final Choices: Making End-of-Life Decisions,
Lee E. Norrgard and Jo DeMars

Healthy Aging, Robin E. Mockenhaupt and
Kathleen Nelson Boyle

Housing Options and Services for Older Adults,
Ann E. Gillespie and Katrinka Smith Sloan

Legal Issues and Older Adults,
Linda Josephson Millman

Mental Health Problems and Older Adults,
Gregory A. Hinrichsen

Older Workers, Sara E. Rix

Paying for Health Care after Age 65,
Elizabeth Vierck

Travel and Older Adults, Allison St. Claire

Volunteerism and Older Adults, Mary K. Kouri

Caregiving of Older Adults

**Louise G. Fradkin
and
Angela Heath**

Choices and Challenges: An Older Adult Reference Series
Elizabeth Vierck, Series Editor

ABC-CLIO
Santa Barbara, California
Denver, Colorado
Oxford, England

Library of Congress Cataloging-in-Publication Data

Fradkin, Louise G., 1927–
    Caregiving of older adults / Louise G. Fradkin and Angela Heath.
        p.   cm. — (Choices and challenges)
    Includes bibliographical references and index.
        1. Aged—Care—United States.   2. Caregivers—Services for—United
    States.   3. Adult children—Services for—United States.   I. Heath,
    Angela.   II. Title.   III. Series.
    HV1461.F68 1992   362.6—dc20   92-34591

ISBN 0-87436-671-2 (alk. paper)

99 98 97 96 95 94   10 9 8 7 6 5 4 3 2

ABC-CLIO, Inc.
130 Cremona Drive, P.O. Box 1911
Santa Barbara, California 93116-1911

This book is printed on acid-free paper ⊗.
Manufactured in the United States of America

Who Am I?

Who am I? My husband died eight years ago so
I am no longer a wife.

Who am I? My grandchildren are all grown and
live miles away. So although I am a
grandmother the role really isn't the same.

Who am I? Twenty years ago I was a teacher, a
productive, responsible person but I've since
then retired.

Who am I? I have a housekeeper come in
everyday so I guess I'm not even a homemaker.

Who am I? I am no longer Leslie's big sister,
nor Calvin's first niece, nor grandpa's first
born because they are all dead.

Who am I? I'm not the snazzy dresser that I
used to be because I have nowhere to go.

Who am I? Who knows? Who cares?

Written by Willa Mae Farley, a 75-year-old
writer, expressing the impact of social
change to her self concept.

Contents

Tables and Figures

Foreword

I have been caring for my 73 year old mother for the past seven years. She is a permanently disabled victim of Multiple Sclerosis (MS) and is confined to a wheelchair. Like most people, neither my mother nor I had given much thought to aging or disability before she was diagnosed with MS at age 59. As I recall the many talks we had had as I was growing up—talks about life, the importance of an education, career, marriage, etc.—never once did either of us bring up the subject of aging and what to do if . . .

Then at 37, the reality of aging—my mother's that is— delivered a hard blow as I watched MS drain the strength, vitality, and independence out of a women who was the epitome of these qualities during her younger, healthier years. Quite suddenly and unexpectedly, our lives were changed, our roles reversed. For the first time in my life, I found myself in unfamiliar territory without a road map or a compass to guide me; I had no battle plan to tell me what to do. The only thing I knew was that my mother had spent her life caring for me. Now she laid helpless, unable to care for herself, and needed me to care for her.

Statistics tell us that there are over seven million people in the United States who shoulder some responsibility for an elderly or disabled family member or friend. As caregivers, we all share common bonds—a desire to see our loved one through difficult times and to provide the best care that we know how. For many of us, this isn't always easy.

Within the pages of *Caregiving of Older Adults*, you will find volumes of information to help you whether you are a caregiver or a professional who works with caregivers. Not only will you find answers to typical concerns about normal aging, diseases most common among the elderly, community resources, housing options, and how to select a nursing home, you will also explore and begin to understand your own mixed emotions as well as those of the older person. In addition, this book contains easy-to-understand information on complicated financial, legal, and insurance issues.

Part two of *Caregiving of Older Adults* is invaluable. This section contains names, addresses, and telephone numbers for helpful national, regional, and state organizations. In addition, each citation explains exactly how the organization may be able to assist you. This will save lots of valuable time and frustration. The glossary defines the terms used by professionals in the field of aging and will help you communicate with them better and the annotated bibliography provides citations for useful, additional reading.

As I look back, I think about how much easier the past seven years of caregiving could have been for me if I had found a resource like *Caregiving of Older Adults*. So much about being a caregiver is often unpredictable. And, this book is organized so that you can go directly to the section that contains information on the issue at hand.

This book is truly one that I recommend highly.

Carolyn Johnson

Carolyn Johnson has been caring for her mother for seven years. She is also founder of Caregivers in Action, an advocacy membership group of caregivers based in Baltimore Maryland. Caregivers in Action provides support to family caregivers through educational seminars, a newsletter, and policy alerts. Caregivers in Action, founded in 1988, advocates for improved home and community-based long term care services and seeks to enhance the ability of caregivers to handle the emotional and physical stress associated with giving care.

Acknowledgments

The authors wish to express their appreciation to Elizabeth Vierck and Tracey Butler for their patience, understanding, and technical input. Our thanks to the librarians of the AARP and NCOA for their help and the use of their resources.

Angela Heath thanks her sister, Carolyn Slade for her technical assistance and quick response to unrealistic deadlines. Many thanks to Warren Brown and Sharon Sellors for expert computer trouble-shooting. And, thanks to Al Smith and Earnest Ingram whose words of encouragement served as a source of inspiration.

Louise Fradkin thanks her husband, Leon, for his encouragement, patience, and immeasurable assistance with the computer. Her thanks to Mirca Liberta for her foresight in co-founding Children of Aging Parents (CAPS) and to all of the caregivers whom CAPS has helped over the past 15 years. Their stories are a part of the background for this book.

How To Use This Book

Each book in the Choices and Challenges series provides a convenient, easy-access reference tool on a specific topic of interest to older adults and those involved with them, including caregivers, spouses, adult children, and gerontology professionals. The books are designed for ease of use, with a generous typeface, ample use of headings and subheadings, and a detailed index.

Each book consists of two parts, which may be used together or independently:

A narrative section providing an informative and comprehensive overview of the topic, written for a lay audience. The narrative can be read straight through or consulted on an as-needed basis by using the headings and subheadings and/or the index.

An annotated resource section that includes a directory of relevant organizations; recommended books, pamphlets, and articles; and software and videos. Where appropriate, the resource section may include additional information relevant to the topic. This section can be used in conjunction with or separately from the narrative to locate sources of additional information, assistance, or support.

A glossary defines important terms and concepts, and the index provides additional access to the material. For easy reference, entries in the resource section are indexed by both topic and title or name.

Introduction

According to the Census Bureau, there are 31 million persons 65 or older. Between 1989 and 2030, the elderly population will double to over 65 million. As equally as astounding as this rapid growth, is the fact that the fastest growing segment of the elderly population is the 75 and older generation, sometimes referred to as the frail elderly. These persons are most likely to need assistance from caregivers, family and friends who provide care, in order to remain in the home.

Providing care to the elderly is not a new phenomenon. Throughout history, there has always been persons willing to assist the less fortunate. Today, however, there are additional social changes and pressures that make caregiving more difficult. First, increased longevity means that Americans are living into advanced age and require more vigorous care. Current caregivers must be skilled at many home nursing procedures that were not required in the past.

In addition, decreased fertility is resulting in fewer children to provide care to aging parents. Likewise, family members are scattered geographically making long distance caregiving an issue for many. And finally, women are entering the labor force in record numbers. Thus, those who find themselves employed outside the home and caregiving at the same time face additional time pressures.

According to AARP, the typical caregiver of the elderly is likely to be female, approximately mid-forties, married, and employed full time outside of the home. Approximately 15 percent of caregivers are over 65. On average, caregivers provide personal care assistance as well as household maintenance chores for 12 hours per week.

The personal and financial costs of giving care can be tremendous. The emotional stress and strain associated with elder caregiving can lead to psychosomatic illnesses, depression, and emotional exhaustion. Forty percent of caregivers incur additional financial expenses for care-related products, services, and activities. On average, caregivers spend about seven percent of their monthly income on these expenses. One-third of working caregivers lose time from work to accommodate the needs of the elderly.

How do caregivers cope? Where do they turn for information and assistance? What kinds of services are available to support them? What can they expect from the older person? Questions such as these are not easily answered and often demand that caregivers struggle through the social service maze in order to identify sources of help. This can be very difficult and time consuming for many caregivers as the needs of most elderly care receivers are multi-faceted and complex.

On the other hand, many caregivers feel that giving care is rewarding. The situation allows them to share precious moments with the care receiver and perhaps to repay them for past efforts. Some caregivers find that this challenge makes them stronger and provides training in valuable life skills.

Regardless of how the caregiving situation is viewed, most caregivers would agree that information and support are vital. *Caregiving of Older Adults* provides caregivers with a roadmap through the many complicated decisions that must be made. It addresses issues of concern such as age-related changes, available services, financial, legal and insurance matters, housing options, and nursing home placement. *Caregiving of Older Adults* will provide caregivers with the information they need and point them in the right direction to obtain further information and assistance.

PART ONE

Caregiving of Older Adults

Chapter 1

Who Are the Informal Caregivers?

Introduction

Caregivers can assume many different roles. They are providers of care, coordinators of care, employers of paid care providers, and planners for future care needs. The term *caregiver* can refer to anyone who provides assistance to someone else who needs it—such as children, older people, disabled individuals, mentally and physically retarded persons, or accident victims. *Informal caregiver* is a term used to refer to unpaid, often untrained individuals such as family members and friends who provide care. *Formal caregivers* are volunteers or paid care providers associated with a service system.

Currently, there is a debate in the professional community regarding when a person should be called an informal caregiver. Some experts believe that a person must provide personal assistance or help with activities of daily living (ADLs) in order to be labeled a caregiver. ADLs are activities that relate to personal self-care such as eating, bathing, dressing, getting in and out of a bed or chair, using the toilet, and moving around inside the home. Other experts maintain that people who assist with instrumental activities of daily living (IADLs) should also be considered caregivers. IADLs are activities associated with managing affairs such as finances, grocery shopping, preparing meals, and housework.

Research suggests that caregiving for the elderly is a process, a continuum of care. Caregiving can start abruptly with the onset of a serious illness such as a heart attack or stroke; or the need for care can begin when a person experiences slight limitations associated with growing older. In the latter case, caregivers may become a little concerned about the person's well-being and offer assistance on occasion. As the older person's limitations become more evident, the caregiver assumes more care-related tasks. If the aging individual becomes severely limited in self-care, caregiving activities become more intense and complicated.

Throughout history, there have always been people available to care for the infirm and the aged. Traditionally, these caregivers have been female, and they have found that, although nurturing can be rewarding, it is also demanding. Many factors contribute to the caregiver's ability to provide care, including the mental and physical health of the older person (the care receiver), the care receiver's attitude, and his or her available financial resources. Other factors contribute to the caregiver's ability and willingness to provide quality care; these include the caregiver's own health; the financial, emotional, and physical support available; conflicting demands on time; and varying coping skills.

The belief that modern families abandon their elders is a myth. Today, most families remain committed to the care of dependent elderly members. Contrary to popular belief, the majority of families do not "put old people away" in nursing homes. At any given time, approximately 5 percent of the older population (people 65 and older) resides in a nursing home. This figure has remained the same for more than a decade. Most older people are cared for by their families and friends until these caregivers are unable to provide the care that is needed. In fact, families provide 70 to 80 percent of the care needed by older people living in the community outside of institutions.

This chapter examines who the caregivers of the elderly are, what they do, the challenges they face, and the coping skills they can employ to make caring a little easier.

FACTS

- Caregivers provide 75 to 80 percent of the care needed by aging adults.

- The median age of caregivers is 45; 28 percent are under 35 years of age and 15 percent are over 65.

- Estimates of the number of caregivers of the elderly in the United States range from 2.2 million to 7 million.

- Approximately 75 percent of caregivers are female.

- One-third of primary caregivers assume the role because they live closest to the older person; another 25 percent state that they had no choice in becoming a caregiver.

Case Study

Lisa, a middle-aged insurance claims representative, has been caring for her mother-in-law for four years. Her mother-in-law, Ida Mae, lives with Lisa and her three children, ages 19, 14, and 7. Lisa has always been close to her mother-in-law and started helping her with chores many years ago. Although Ida Mae has five adult children, four of them live more than 200 miles away. She has always trusted Lisa and preferred asking her for help.

Four years ago when Ida Mae's husband died, she was unprepared to handle the household finances. Lisa began paying her bills, helping with grocery shopping, and arranging for minor household repairs. Nine months later, Ida Mae suffered a series of ministrokes that left her paralyzed on one side and slightly disoriented at times. Lisa worked with a discharge planner at the hospital to arrange for a home-health aide and a physical therapist. For two months, Lisa experienced problems with aides who did not come to work on time or did not show up at all. Lisa was frequently late for work and had to use company time to telephone the home-health agency.

Two and a half years ago, Ida Mae moved in with Lisa and her family because she had become more disoriented and was unable to bathe, groom, and prepare meals without assistance. All the family members took turns caring for Ida Mae. The children often resented taking time away from their recreational activities to care for their grandmother. They were embarrassed by Ida Mae's inappropriate behavior and mood swings.

One year ago, Lisa discovered that her husband was having an affair, and she filed for a divorce. The divorce became final last month. Nonetheless, Lisa still cares for her former mother-in-law in her home. She receives financial assistance from her ex-husband and his brothers and sisters, but Lisa is left to perform the day-to-day caregiving chores alone, with the help of her children and a part-time home-health aide.

This case study highlights the dynamics of the American family in a caregiving situation. Of Ida Mae's five children, only one lives in close proximity. Today's society is a mobile one; it is not uncommon for parents and adult children to live in different cities and states. Consequently, fewer family members are geographically available to give care to an elder. Relatives who live closest to the older person in need are likely to become caregivers. According to the American Association of Retired Persons (AARP), one-third of primary caregivers assume the role because they live close to the older person.

Lisa is one of the many caregivers who are part of the sandwich generation, those adults who are providing care to both children and older relatives. As more women delay childbearing, the likelihood of this situation increases. And, like 55 percent of all caregivers, Lisa is employed outside the home. The added pressures of caring for children and meeting job demands can cause time conflicts and lead to physical exhaustion for caregivers.

Divorce can also complicate caregiving. As many women care for their in-laws, a divorce may interrupt or discontinue the care being provided. Likewise, children of divorced parents may find it difficult to give care as a result of family conflicts. And caregivers who divorce without having children and who do not remarry are without the benefit of support.

The art of caring is changing. Not only is the number of older people needing care increasing; the complexity of their needs is also intensifying. Unfortunately, the resources available to meet these needs are decreasing. Some experts predict that current societal trends, such as lower fertility rates, the larger number of women in the labor force, and declining federal spending on social programs, will decrease the availability of caregivers. Other experts believe that caregivers will continue to provide care, yet experience a decrease in personal life satisfaction.

Personal Challenges

Caregivers face a number of challenges. These include learning basic health care skills; coping with physical, emotional, and financial stress; understanding legal options; accessing the service system; and learning how to balance conflicting demands while dealing with potentially stressful family dynamics.

Some caregivers handle these challenges better than others. Caregiving responsibilities can lead to feelings of love, generosity, and a strengthening of family ties. Some caregivers are thankful for the opportunity to provide care and to share in the final days of the older person's life.

For others, these responsibilities can be overwhelming and lead to isolation, physical illness, financial devastation, and loss of employment. In severe cases, caregiver exhaustion can lead to elder abuse—the financial exploitation, neglect, or mental or physical abuse of an older person.

FACTS

- Caregivers provide assistance for an average of approximately 12 hours per week; 28 percent give care for 8 hours or less, while 36 percent provide help for 21 hours or more.

- Two-thirds of caregivers assist older people with ADLs or personal care.

- Caregiving causes 68 percent of caregivers to spend less time on leisure; 57 percent have been unable to take a vacation; and 43 percent spend less time with family members and pay less attention to their own health.

- Approximately 39 percent of caregivers of the elderly also have children at home.

- Some 55 percent of caregivers are also employed outside the home, 42 percent full-time and 13 percent part-time.

Caregiver Tasks

On average, caregivers provide assistance 12 hours per week. The older person's level of need for support can vary by activity. For example, a person may require only supervision to complete a number of tasks, need actual help to complete other tasks, and be incapable of performing yet other activities. Caregivers are cautioned not to perpetuate learned helplessness by providing a more intense level of support than is actually needed. Although the care receiver may take a longer time to complete an activity or perhaps perform it poorly, older people should be encouraged to care for themselves. In doing so, they maintain their drive and sense of independence.

Tables 1.1 and 1.2 depict the areas of support most frequently provided by caregivers. Many caregivers perform personal care services; approximately 68 percent assist with one or more ADLs. Approximately 19 percent assist with one ADL, 15 percent with two ADLs, and 33 percent assist with three more ADLs. Almost all caregivers perform one or more IADLs.

Generally, male and female caregivers provide different types of care to older people. Men typically perform traditionally male tasks such as providing transportation, household repair, and financial management or support. However, many men fully participate in all types of caregiving tasks. Women, on the other hand, typically provide assistance with personal hygiene and household tasks.

In addition to ADL and IADL supports, caregivers coordinate social services. This role can involve identifying support systems, completing applications, monitoring services provided, and identifying new supports as the needs change. Coordinating the

Table 1.1   Percentage of Caregivers Providing ADL Assistance

walking	46%
dressing	41%
bathing	38%
toileting	29%
eating	27%
0 — 20 — 40 — 60 — 80 — 100	

Taken from the National Survey of Caregivers: Final Report, AARP, November 1988.

Table 1.2   Percentage of Caregivers Providing IADL Assistance

grocery shopping	83%
transportation	79%
housework	75%
meals preparation	68%
managing finances	65%
administering medicine	45%
0 — 20 — 40 — 60 — 80 — 100	

Taken from the National Survey of Caregivers: Final Report, AARP, November 1988.

formal system can be very frustrating and time-consuming for caregivers who are uninformed about the service delivery system.

Stress—Physical, Emotional, and Financial

Caregiving can be a very stressful occupation. If stress continues over a prolonged period of time, it can lead to caregiver burnout, a state of exhaustion that has negative consequences for both the caregiver and the care receiver. Caregiver burnout has three components, according to the New York State Department on Aging:

- Emotional exhaustion   A depletion of emotional resources, creating a feeling that one has nothing left to give.

- Depersonalization   The development of negative or insensitive attitudes about the care receiver.

- Reduced personal accomplishment   A devalued sense of self, resulting in a feeling that there is nothing beyond caregiving.

PHYSICAL STRESS

The physical demands of caregiving can be grueling. According to the National Survey of Caregivers, one-fourth of care receivers either are bedridden or use wheelchairs. People caring for these individuals must physically lift the person several times a day. Constant lifting can cause muscle strain and back problems, particularly for caregivers who have not been trained in proper lifting techniques.

Another source of physical stress is sleep deprivation. The nature of some illnesses can cause the care receiver to have poor sleeping habits. The older person may awaken several times during the night because of pain, the need to urinate, or disorientation. Alzheimer's disease patients have a tendency to wander around the house during the night. Disruptive sleep patterns can exhaust the caregiver and lead to disorientation, physical illness, and irritability on his or her part.

Physical fatigue can also be caused by mental stress, worry, and excessive travel in the case of long-distance caregiving.

Physical demands and stress can be detrimental for caregivers, many of whom are middle-aged and older and have their own health concerns. However, caregivers have a tendency to overlook their own medical conditions. In fact, 33 percent report paying less attention to personal health since becoming caregivers.

EMOTIONAL STRESS

When people speak about the stresses of caregiving, they are often referring to the mixed emotions that plague many caregivers. It is important to note that some caregivers do not experience difficulties in this role and regard it as a pleasant one with only mild irritations. A person's attitude and ability to cope with stress directly affect the reaction to difficult caregiving scenarios. In the words of one caregiver, "Caregiving, like life, is a series of problem-solving techniques. Some of us are good at it and some of us are not."

There are numerous reasons why caregivers are faced with conflicting emotions. First, the role of a caregiver is an ambiguous one. There are no guidelines that specify what is to be done and how. Caring for a person with multiple debilitating illnesses demands skills that many caregivers do not possess. Unfortunately, most people in this situation have not been exposed to training programs that teach the mechanics of giving care. Often, there is no time to prepare for the role.

Second, past family conflicts and poor communication patterns have a direct impact on a person's ability and willingness to give care. It is unrealistic to think that hurtful disagreements can be dismissed once the need for care arises. And once caregiving begins, new conflicts can develop.

Third, balancing caregiving responsibilities with personal needs, employment, and the needs of a spouse or children can be very difficult. Some have referred to caregiving as the ultimate juggling act, whereby the caregiver must balance multiple responsibilities simultaneously. Any sudden change in the condition of the older person can adversely affect one's ability to maintain balance. Readjustments are needed frequently, and inevitably some needs may go unmet due to time constraints.

Caregivers report experiencing a variety of emotions.

Guilt

Guilt is one of the most common emotions experienced by caregivers. There are numerous reasons why caregivers feel guilty. These feelings are often produced by unfulfilled expectations—whether self-imposed or the expectations of others. Many people regret past events within relationships. Such regrets can intensify for caregivers as they watch the older person decline. They feel guilty for wanting to forego caregiving responsibilities, yet also experience guilt for allowing others to give support. Guilt may also arise when one is short-tempered with the older person, wants to spend time with family and friends, or expresses negative attitudes about the older person.

Grief and Loss

Watching someone slowly deteriorate or suffer is very painful. It is difficult to witness a strong, independent person becoming reduced to a frail, helpless individual. The grief of a spousal caregiver may be overwhelming because the well spouse is losing a life companion. Adult children feel a deep sense of loss as they watch their parents, previously authoritative and capable, slowly lose their abilities.

Some caregivers may grieve because the joys and activities shared in the past are no longer available. Others grieve over the impending death of the older person. But for all, the experience of being a care provider elicits feelings concerning the frailty of life and one's own aging.

Isolation

Caregivers feel alone. Such a total investment of time and energy in another person's life can cause a loss of self-identity. In many cases, the demands of the situation prevent caregivers from participating in recreational and social activities. In situations where the care receiver is unable to provide companionship, the loneliness can be intense. In addition to physical isolation, caregivers may feel an emotional distance from others who do not understand their concerns. Caregivers who are unable to express concerns have greater feelings of loneliness.

Exhaustion and Helplessness

Many caregivers constantly feel there are too many things that need to be done and they do not know where to start. Caregivers' beliefs can contribute to their being overwhelmed, or these feelings can be created by others. For example, some people attempt to be "super caregivers" and accomplish demanding tasks alone. They perceive that no one else can "do their job" and often do more for the older person than is actually required. Other people may expect attention at the same time that the older person insists that the caregiver address a need. Some caregivers find it impossible to say no to conflicting demands.

In addition, a feeling of helplessness exists because the caregiver cannot control the older person's illnesses and limitations. Caregivers would like to be able to reverse the situation. But in reality, many times the only thing they can do is respond to the changes as they occur.

Anger

In most caregiving situations, anger comes and goes. Caregivers get angry at themselves, the older person, others involved in providing care, and those who do not provide care. They get angry at themselves for being unable to demand time for themselves. They resent the care receiver for being a burden and seeming ungrateful. Others who do not perform care-related tasks according to caregivers' expectations may become targets of their anger, and they get furious at people who seem selfish and refuse to give help.

Embarrassment

Sometimes care receivers exhibit embarrassing behavior. This is particularly true for Alzheimer's disease patients. These patients may wander outside half-dressed, play with food, or urinate in public. Family members are embarrassed by such inappropriate behavior. In some cases, the embarrassment is so strong that the caregiver attempts to isolate the older person.

Dutifulness

Most family caregivers feel that they have a moral obligation to provide for the aging family member or spouse. These older relatives have frequently provided the caregiver with care, love, and assistance in the past. Caregiving represents an opportunity to repay elders.

Love and Joy

Many caregivers have very endearing memories of the older person. These loving feelings give them the strength to continue providing care. Caring for the elder creates a sense of joy, especially when the care receiver is pleasant and grateful. However, loving feelings can also lead to inappropriate promises, like swearing "never to put you in a nursing home," though a time may come when the caregiver is unable to provide the needed care. Loving feelings may also prevent the caregiver from letting others assist with caring.

Closeness

The need for care can bring the caregiver and the older person closer together. Some caregivers have mastered the skill of reminiscing, sharing hopes and dreams, telling jokes, and simply enjoying the older person's company while providing personal care. Caregiving presents an opportunity to express positive feelings that may have never been shared.

Pride and Thankfulness

Caregivers often feel thankful that the relative has lived to a ripe old age. Many take pride in the capabilities the older person still possesses. They are proud of being caregivers and feel they are doing an excellent job.

The important thing to remember about these varied, sometimes conflicting, feelings is that they are all normal. Feelings change from day to day and maybe even from hour to hour depending on the circumstances. Usually, the caregiver experiences more than one emotion at the same time. Caregivers should avoid being intensely preoccupied with conflicting emotions. If emotions become too much to bear, caregivers are encouraged to seek professional counseling or support groups.

FINANCIAL STRESS

In addition to performing care-related activities, caregiving can also have an economic consequence. About 60 percent of caregivers incur out-of-pocket expenses. The most frequent costs are travel, telephone bills, special diets and medicine, and doctors' fees. Only a small number of caregivers incur the most costly expenses, those for hospital or home care. For those who incur health-related expenses, the monthly averages are $275 for hospital care, $238 for home nursing, $83 for respite care, and $76 for homemakers. But on the average, caregivers incur total monthly expenses of $117, or about 7 percent of the typical caregiver's monthly income.

There are limited opportunities for recouping out-of-pocket expenses. However, most states offer two strategies to offset caregiver expenditures: direct payments and tax allowances. As of 1986, 35 states offered direct payments to those providing home care. Typically, only those caring for elderly people at risk of institutionalization are eligible. In 1988, 28 states had tax provisions for elder dependent care. Eligibility criteria vary, and consumers should contact their state tax departments for particulars.

Some federal income tax provisions assist older people and their caregivers. People over age 65 receive a higher federal, and sometimes state, exemption rate. They may also qualify to receive federal credit for elderly or disabled persons, based on their income. Some caregivers can apply for child and dependent care credit, which allows employed families to deduct up to $2,400 for elder care expenses from federal income tax. In order to qualify for the tax credit, the elder must be considered the taxpayer's dependent, according to the U.S. Internal Revenue Service (IRS) definition. The IRS uses the following criteria to stipulate whether an older person can be claimed as a dependent:

> The older person must spend at least eight hours in the caregiver's home.

> The older person must be incapable of self-care.

> The caregiver is responsible for 51 percent of the care receiver's expenses.

Such restrictive criteria make it virtually impossible for many caregivers to take advantage of the tax credit. Similarly, the credit is not refundable, that is, the amount of the credit cannot exceed the total tax liability of a taxpayer. Thus, many low-income caregivers are not eligible.

Time Constraints

Today's society operates at an accelerated pace. Numerous demands create conflicting time constraints for caregivers, leading to anxiety for many as they attempt to fulfill family, civic, and job responsibilities. Consequently, the additional pressures of caring for an older person can lead to exhaustion, anger, and illness.

How do caregivers balance the demands on their time? Many find this very difficult and feel pressured because some tasks must go undone. Typically, caregivers attempt to meet the demands of others and delay or forget about personal needs. According to the National Survey of Caregivers, 51 percent spend less time on leisure activities, 34 percent spend less time with their families, and 28 percent have been unable to take a vacation since becoming caregivers. Caring for an Alzheimer's patient is extremely time-consuming and has been referred to as the 36-hour day.

EMPLOYMENT

Some 55 percent of caregivers are also employed outside the home. Companies, researchers, program planners, and the media have begun paying attention to the plight of employed caregivers. Numerous studies indicate that caregiving affects employment. Companies report that employee caregivers are tardy and absent from work more often, experience decreased productivity, and use the company telephone for personal reasons more often than other workers. Several studies suggest that the stress experienced by working caregivers leads to more frequent use of company health benefits.

Caregiving may also involve several hidden costs. Some caregivers choose early retirement, switch from full-time to part-time work, or do not pursue promotions in order to devote more time to an older relative. The immediate consequence is decreased income and loss of benefits. This is particularly disturbing to low-income caregivers and middle-aged people who find private health insurance policies to be unaffordable. In addition, these caregivers are likely to decrease their opportunity to achieve pension-vesting rights, and thus they earn decreased retirement income.

Gradually employers are beginning to provide workers with support. Company support for working caregivers includes information and counseling, direct services, and benefits.

Corporations most frequently offer information and counseling. The IBM Elder Care Referral Service is a model for companies interested in offering a national information and referral network. IBM employees can telephone 175 local information organizations to help clarify their needs and receive referrals to appropriate services. Less expensive information and counseling models include production of employee handbooks on caregiving, lunchtime educational seminars, and employee assistance programs (EAPs), which assist employees with their personal problems.

Very few companies provide direct services. The Stride Rite Corporation recently opened a model intergenerational day-care center in the corporate headquarters. The center provides care for both children and dependent elders during working hours. Some companies also offer support groups for caregivers, typically during lunchtime. In addition, a few retiree groups provide long-term care services to frail members.

Many American companies offer benefits that are helpful, although not specifically designed to address caregiver needs. For example, flextime, part-time work, and work-at-home options allow caregivers flexibility during the day. Benefits designed specifically for caregivers of the young and the old include dependent-care leave, dependent-care assistance programs (DCAP), and long-term care insurance.

There are various dependent-care leave programs. Policies allow employees to take time away from work to care for a sick child, spouse, or parent. Most programs grant leaves for up to three months without pay. However, American Telephone & Telegraph, Inc. (AT&T) allows employees to take up to 12 months of unpaid leave. Basic health insurance, medical, and dental benefits continue at the company's expense. DCAP programs are offered by approximately 1,100 employers. This benefit allows employees to set aside up to $5,000 of pretax income on an annual basis to pay for child and elderly care. The company holds the money in an account and issues it to the employee as expenses are incurred. Long-term care insurance is less frequently available, offered by only 153 employers as of 1990. In most cases, the employee pays the entire group rate premium.

Family Dynamics

The typical family experiences some conflicts and disagreements. A crisis situation such as caregiving can elicit old, hurt feelings and unreconciled differences. The caregiver is sometimes in conflict with the care receiver, siblings, spouse, children, and other family members because each has a different perspective and approach to handling the situation.

On the other hand, the need to give care to an older family member may bring the family together. A crisis often causes family members to work in concert to address issues of concern. Family members may improve communication with each other in an attempt to make joint decisions, thereby increasing understanding of one another. A deeper sensitivity toward family members can evolve, leading to more satisfying relationships.

Caring for an older person affects the entire family, but not all members are affected in the same way. Although each family situation is different, generally the immediate family of the primary caregiver must make adjustments, even young children. Caregiving demands a reallocation of family resources, time spent together, and household chores. And, although caregivers share many of the same responsibilities, concerns, and conflicts, different types of caregivers—spouses, adult children, and long-distance caregivers—face unique challenges.

Spousal Caregivers

Many older couples have shared life for decades. Disability of either can be devastating to both spouses, even when relations are not close. In addition, the spousal caregiver is often dealing with personal health concerns associated with aging. For most of today's older males, a wife is a confidant; for most older females, a husband is a decision maker. Changes in the way spouses relate are difficult for many. Inevitably, spousal caregiving changes marital responsibilities. Wives find themselves in the unfamiliar position of making decisions about family finances. Husbands may be faced with learning how to perform household chores.

The moral obligation to care for a spouse is related to the marriage vows to love and honor "in sickness and in health, till death do us part." Consequently, spousal caregivers may be less inclined to define themselves as caregivers and thus resist seeking assistance. A husband or a wife may view caregiving as a part of the marital duties. As a result, spouses may be very uncomfortable voicing feelings of anger or frustration.

In most cases, due to the longer life expectancy of women, the wife provides care for the husband. One national survey reports that 23 percent of caregivers are wives and 13 percent are husbands. For some men, being a care receiver causes feelings of humiliation, especially when limitations are severe. A husband may feel less manly as a result. For some wives, needing care is equally humiliating, especially when the husband must complete household chores. For each spouse, caregiving demands adjustment.

Adult Children

Daughters are most often the caregivers of their parents with 29 percent of all caregivers being daughters. In fact, some experts refer to the dutiful daughter syndrome to describe caregivers who are overburdened. Sons, on the other hand, compose about 9 percent of all caregivers. Sons, like other male caregivers, most often assist with instrumental activities of daily living such as running errands, financial management, and household repair.

Most children feel a sense of duty or filial responsibility toward their parents, even though the parent–child relationship may have been strained in the past. The expectation that children care for a frail parent can be traced back at least to colonial days. *Exploding the Myths: Caregiving in America* cites a historical document quoting an eighteenth-century preacher as warning: "Children that have been the charge of their parents to bring them up to be capable of doing something, should not presently, in hopes of doing better for themselves, desert their helpless parent, as thinking it is time for themselves and let them shift as they can." The sense of duty also has a religious basis; one of the Ten Commandments instructs children to "honor thy mother and thy father."

When the health or mental status of a parent declines drastically, adult children experience uncomfortable feelings of role reversal. That is, the parent becomes dependent on the adult child, who assumes more of a leadership position. These feelings are difficult for both generations; the situation does not feel normal. The parent may attempt to maintain independence, while the adult child is struggling to do what is believed to be best for the parent.

The care needed by aging parents can cause problems within the adult child's family. If married, adult children are caught between the needs of parents and loyalty to their spouses. This can be difficult if the older person is extremely needy or the spouse is not understanding. In addition, the adult's own children may be affected by caregiving. Grandparents are viewed as a source of joy as well as a source of irritation by many children who participate in caregiving. Some grandchildren may feel neglected because the older person seems to be the focus of the parent's attention.

Other family members are also affected when the caregiver is an adult child. Sibling rivalry may continue or intensify when the parent becomes dependent. There may be unfilled expectations or disagreements about the approach to providing care.

Long-Distance Caregivers

People with ailing parents who live at a distance have some unique concerns. Giving care from a distance can cause anxiety, financial strain, and confusion in the attempt to identify needs and coordinate care. Long-distance caregivers are faced with two options: They can coordinate care from a distance or move the older person closer.

Coordinating Care from a Distance

Knowing the needs of an older person who lives in a distant city or state is difficult. Although the caregiver may keep in touch by telephone, the extent of problems may be vaguely understood. Older people may not express their limitations or they may exaggerate their conditions. People living in the same community with the older person can be solicited to monitor the elder's well-being and report to the caregiver when there is a problem.

During visits, caregivers can observe as the older person completes everyday activities and notice changes in appearance, eating habits, socialization patterns, and emotional stability. If the caregiver suspects that the older person needs assistance, the Checklist of Concerns/Resources for Caregivers, found in Chapter 3 (page 51), is a good tool to help focus discussions about areas of concern. Caregivers must keep in mind that their perceptions may differ from the older person's. The elder may be willing to cope with minor inconveniences in order to maintain independence. The older person's wishes should be respected as long as he or she is mentally capable of making decisions and there is no threat to safety.

To locate services to meet the needs identified, the caregiver should first contact the local department on aging. Chapter 3 contains further information about services available in many communities and how to gain access to the service system.

When the older person has multiple needs, or the caregiver does not have time to locate social programs, the services of a private geriatric care manager may prove beneficial. Case managers evaluate the older person's situation, identify appropriate services, and maintain contact with the out-of-town caregiver. Private geriatric care managers can be located by contacting the National Association of Private Geriatric Care Managers or Aging Network Services listed in Chapter 8. Caregivers can also refer to *Case Management Resource Guide,* a reference book available in most local libraries.

Relocating

Many long-distance caregivers consider relocating the older person when a crisis occurs. It is important to remember that most older people prefer living independently and often reject the idea of moving in with relatives or friends. Relocating to an unfamiliar environment can be disorienting and isolating for older people.

Sharing a household with a care receiver can be gratifying, but it can also be destructive, affecting the entire family. The family considering combining households with an older relative may want to discuss how each person feels about the move, whether other alternatives are more appropriate, and the anticipated future needs of the older person. Flexibility is necessary to accommodate the numerous adjustments and readjustments. Caregivers should consider how space will be utilized and privacy maintained, how each family member will contribute to caring and making schedule modifications, and how family finances will be affected.

Family Meetings

Family meetings are an effective method of providing the opportunity for all concerned to share in decisions regarding the care of older members. By discussing concerns openly, the family may be able to eliminate or lessen disagreement. Although the entire family may not agree on all issues, individual members can suggest alternative approaches to problem solving, which stimulates creative exchanges and better decision making.

All family members should participate in the meeting, including children. It is important to include the older person and allow him or her to maintain some sense of control. Relatives who live at a distance can participate by telephone or by providing a written position statement on issues to be discussed.

Each person attending should receive a written agenda prior to the meeting that outlines the purpose of the meeting, what is to be accomplished, and how decisions will be ratified. Participants should agree to ground rules such as honesty, willingness to listen to each other, and keeping the best interests of the older person in mind. Members can decide on medical treatment, financial management, living arrangements, contributions by each member, and legal matters. The family should continue having conferences once or twice a year, or when a crisis arises.

Family conference may be difficult or impossible in some situations. Disagreements during the past may preclude certain members from participating. It might be helpful to have an impartial professional such as a family therapist or social worker facilitate the meeting.

Coping Skills

There are many things a caregiver can do to cope with caregiving. Many caregivers are so involved in providing for the aging person that they neglect themselves; however, caregivers must realize the importance of self-care. Self-care is a right and a requirement to assure the continued provision of quality care.

Following are several strategies for dealing with stress:

- Set limits   It is vital to identify what can be done comfortably. Do not take on more than you can handle. Plan respite breaks and learn to say no.

- Accept help from others   Realize that other people want to help. Delegate responsibilities; accepting help from others is healthy. Encourage the older person to participate in self-care.

- Deal with conflicting emotions   Accept these feelings as normal, typical, human reactions to caregiving. Seek a counselor or support group, if needed.

- Maintain outside involvements   Do not allow caregiving to become all-consuming. Find ways to participate in interesting activities. Write letters, use the telephone, stay in touch.

- Learn to relax   Find activities that are relaxing. Many community agencies teach relaxation techniques. There are also video and audiocassette programs.

- Monitor your own health   It is important to eat properly, exercise regularly, get enough sleep, and keep medical appointments. If possible, discontinue negative life-style habits such as smoking and drinking.

- Practice time-management techniques   Organize time more efficiently. Identify tasks to be done, rank order them in terms of importance, and eliminate nonessential activities. Complete what is possible during the time available, and leave the rest until tomorrow. Pace yourself so that you can continue providing care for as long as possible.

References

American Association of Retired Persons (AARP). *Miles Away and Still Caring: A Guide for Long-Distance Caregivers*. Washington, DC: AARP, 1986.

AARP and Administration on Aging. *A Profile of Older Americans 1990*. Washington, DC: AARP, 1990.

AARP. *A National Survey of Caregivers: Final Report*. Washington, DC: AARP, 1988.

Couper, Donna P. *Aging and Our Families: Handbook for Family Caregivers*. New York: Human Sciences Press, 1989.

Heath, Angela. "The American Corporate Response to Caregiving of Elders." *Aging International* 17, no. 2 (Winter 1990): 43–47.

Hess, Beth B., and Elizabeth W. Markson, eds. *Growing Old in America*. New Brunswick, NJ: Transaction Publishers, 1991.

New York State Office for the Aging. *Caregivers Practical Help*. Buffalo, NY: New York State Department on Aging, 1987.

Springer, Dianne, and Timothy H. Brubaker. *Family Caregivers and Dependent Elderly: Minimizing Stress and Maximizing Independence*. Beverly Hills, CA: Sage Publications, 1984.

U.S. Congress. House. Select Committee on Aging. *Exploding the Myths: Caregiving in America* Committee publication no. 100-665. Washington, DC: GPO, August 1988.

Chapter 2

Understanding the Care Receiver

Introduction

Today's society is youth-oriented. Americans spend billions of dollars each year attempting to delay aging. In fact, aging as a field of study is still in its infancy. Scientists and researchers began to explore the differences between normal and abnormal aging only about three decades ago.

Nonetheless, most Americans know little about normal aging. Most see old age is a time to be feared, a time that represents limitations and illnesses. The belief that old age is a season of losses is prevalent.

It is a fact that the human body changes with increasing age. Yet the effects of aging vary from person to person. There are biological, environmental, health, and life-style factors that contribute to the impact of the aging process on the individual. Likewise, a person's attitude helps determine his or her reactions to growing older. In most cases, people are able to compensate for the changes that occur.

Social changes are also common as a person ages. Growing older brings on retirement, the death of loved ones, and decreased mobility. Changes in social patterns can lead to isolation, loneliness, and a devalued sense of self. For many older people, social changes are far more devastating than normal physical decline.

Caregivers need to be aware of the many changes experienced by elderly care receivers. Understanding the normal aging process will help assure that abnormal conditions are examined further. And understanding the emotional, social, and psychological consequences of aging will help the caregiver empathize with the older person's actions and reactions. This chapter explores the changes associated with aging and the ways older people and their caregivers can compensate for these limitations.

FACTS

- There are 31 million people in the United States over age 65, approximately 12.5 percent of the population.

- Average life expectancy in 1900 was 47 years; in 1990 it was 75.

- By 2030, approximately 22 percent of the U.S. population will be 65 or older.

- In 1989, about 10 percent of people 65 and older were members of a minority group.

Demographics

The United States, like all Western countries, is graying. This country is experiencing a dramatic increase in the number and percentage of older people in the population. In 1990, there were 31 million people over age 65, about one in every eight Americans, or 12.5 percent of the population. This unprecedented number of elderly people is more apparent when compared with figures from previous years. In the early 1900s, about 3.1 million people, or 4.1 percent of the population, lived to see old age. By 1940, that figure had increased to 9 million. And since 1980, the number of elderly Americans has risen from 25.7 million by 5.3 million, or 21 percent.

The older population itself is aging. People age 75 and above are the fastest growing segment of the population. In 1989, there were 9.8 million Americans in the 75–84 age group and 3 million people 85 years of age or older. Today, life expectancy at birth is about 75 years. However, average life expectancy for someone who is 65 now is almost 82, or 84 years for women and 80 years for men. In 1990, there were about 37,360 centenarians, people age 100 and over, up from 3,000 in 1960.

The older population is expected to continue growing. The most rapid increase will occur as the baby boomers (those born between 1947 and 1964) begin to age. The over-65 population is expected to increase from 39.4 million in 2010 to 65.6 million by 2030. By 2030, one in five Americans will be elderly.

Physical Changes

With age, many body functions decline. This decline is very gradual and often is not noticed until one is between 30 and 40 years of age. In general, older people have learned how to compensate for many of the physical changes experienced throughout the years. Nevertheless, for some, physical decline is traumatic.

Case Studies

CASE ONE

Mrs. Williams is a cheerful, 78-year-old African-American woman who lives alone in her apartment. Mrs. Williams has been diagnosed with multiple conditions including arthritis, high blood pressure, inner ear imbalance, and poor circulation. Her eyesight is failing, yet her hearing is still very keen. She has trouble walking and standing for long periods of time. But Mrs. Williams has learned to compensate for her disabilities and is still able to care for herself without much assistance.

When Mrs. Williams awakes in the morning, her muscles are very stiff and painful. She slowly gets out of bed, stretching and flexing her arms and legs to loosen the stiffness. She uses several assistive devices including a walker, a shower chair, and a raised toilet seat. She prepares her own meals but needs to sit in order to check foods baking in the oven. Every day, Mrs. Williams cleans her apartment, sews quilts for her social club, and talks to friends on the telephone. She relies on her daughter for grocery shopping and other errands because she cannot walk long distances and never learned how to drive.

CASE TWO

Mr. Jacobs is a depressed, 71-year-old white man who lives alone in his apartment. Mr. Jacobs suffers from arthritis, poor circulation, and diabetes. Mr. Jacobs's hearing is failing, yet his sight is still good. Mr. Jacobs has not learned to compensate for his disabilities and is bitter about his situation.

In the morning when he awakes, a home-health aide helps him with bathing, dressing, and preparing meals. Although he has a cane and a hearing aid, he refuses to use either. He spends most of his day, in between naps, staring blankly at the television set. He has no hobbies and does not attempt to keep in contact with friends. He relies on his family to manage his finances and run errands.

These case studies highlight the different ways older individuals may react to similar disabilities and the importance of attitude in making adjustments. Mrs. Williams seems to accept her limitations and has a positive attitude toward problem solving. She is fiercely independent and prefers to remain socially involved. On the other hand, Mr. Jacobs appears to be depressed, perhaps because he is no longer able to enjoy the life-style he had when he was younger. He makes little attempt to participate in self-care or social activities. Although Mrs. Williams is seven years older than Mr. Jacobs, her attitude makes her seem twenty years younger.

Sensory Changes

Aging causes deficits in each of the five senses. Changes in vision and hearing are the most pronounced. Sensory decline distorts one's ability to interact with the environment. Sensory degeneration can lead to communication problems, an inability to detect danger, and sometimes isolation.

VISION

Receiving adequate visual cues is important for social interaction and self-care. As people grow older, their visual acuity declines. Some 30 percent of older people have poor vision by age 80.

Older people are less likely to see well in a dimly lit atmosphere because their pupils have decreased in size. On the other hand, glare is particularly disturbing because it can cause momentary blindness and lead to accidents. Also, as the lenses of the eyes lose elasticity, elderly people are less able to focus on near objects, and the ability to shift focus from near to far and from light to dark decreases.

A caregiver can help the older person cope with visual changes. The first step is to encourage the care receiver to have annual eye examinations. Be sure to have the older person tested for common disorders like glaucoma and cataracts. Glaucoma is caused by pressure in the eye and can lead to blindness. Cataracts, the increased clouding of the lens, can be surgically removed.

If glasses are prescribed, help the older person select attractive frames that are complimentary to the person's facial features. And if the older person has night blindness, an inability to see at night, suggest that he or she refrain from driving at night. Remember that sometimes an older person is unable to identify things or people and may appear to be disoriented, while in actuality the problem is visual.

The environment can be modified to compensate for visual loss. Increasing direct light and eliminating glare will promote better sight. Glare is decreased by avoiding high-gloss waxes on floor surfaces and furniture and by shading large window panes. Sunglasses and hats also cut down on glare in bright sunlight or snow. The colors red and yellow can be used to identify objects and to outline floor level changes and steps. Walkways and stairs should be cleared of protruding objects. Chapter 5 contains further information on how to modify a home.

HEARING

Presbycusis is a common, irreversible hearing loss associated with aging. It is caused by changes in the inner ear, and it creates difficulty in distinguishing between similar sounds and an inability to hear high pitches. Hearing difficulty is often worsened by distracting background noises or multiple conversations. People often presume that hearing aids are appropriate for all types of hearing loss. But many hearing aids are not effective for presbycusis because they amplify all sound, including background noises, and may further distort hearing.

If hearing problems occur, the caregiver should encourage the older person to have a hearing evaluation performed by an audiologist. The audiologist will identify the extent and nature of the hearing loss and recommend appropriate action.

In communicating with elderly people who have hearing difficulties, caregivers can practice the following tips identified by the New York State Department on Aging:

* Never cover your mouth, mumble, or eat while speaking.
* Get the older person's attention before starting to talk.

- Speak slightly louder and a little more slowly than to people with good hearing.

- Lower the tone of your voice.

- Reduce background noises, if possible.

- Do not speak from a distance greater than 6 feet.

- Speak to the person's better ear.

- Use short, concise sentences.

TASTE, SMELL, AND TOUCH

Changes in the senses of taste, smell, and feeling are less noticeable than changes in vision and hearing. The number of taste buds declines as people grow older, decreasing the ability to taste salts and sugar. This limitation is sometimes aggravated by medications or dentures.

Researchers believe that the sense of smell also decreases slightly with advanced age. Declining abilities to taste and smell can sometimes make food taste bland. The sense of feeling also diminishes slightly with age. As a result, older people are less aware of changes in temperatures.

To a limited extent, caregivers can help older people compensate for the effects of changes in these three senses. Caregivers can enhance the taste of food by using herbs and spices, presenting meals in a pleasant arrangement, and keeping dentures clean. Smoke detectors should be checked regularly since older people may not smell smoke. And caregivers can make sure that the care receiver dresses appropriately for the weather to avoid hypothermia (low body temperatures) and hyperthermia (heat stroke).

Prevalent Illnesses

Multiple health concerns are a reality for many older people. In fact, four out of five older people have at least one chronic illness. Despite the various illnesses afflicting the elderly, the majority are able to live in the community with the help of social supports. The following information on common illnesses experienced by older people includes tips for caregivers.

Heart Problems

Heart disease is one of the most common causes of death for the elderly. Angina, or chest pain resulting from poor blood circulation to the heart muscles, is frightening and uncomfortable. It can be caused by a blockage in the artery leading to the heart, uncontrolled high blood pressure, or hardening of the arteries. The pain caused by angina is often described as a squeezing pain that affects the left side of the chest, shoulder, and arm. Angina is often brought on by situations that stress the heart, such as physical exertion or an emotional upset. Angina is a warning sign that the heart muscles are being overburdened.

Congestive heart failure (CHF) is a backup of blood in the heart and other organs. CHF of the left heart muscle results in lung congestion and CHF of the right heart muscle causes congestion in the liver. These disorders arise from damaged heart muscles and heart valves, mechanisms that control the flow of blood through the heart. Symptoms of CHF include shortness of breath after slight exertion or lying down, swelling of the abdomen and ankles, and abnormal fatigue.

A heart attack, also known as a coronary vascular occlusion, occurs when the heart muscle does not receive an adequate blood supply, causing muscle tissue to die. Symptoms of a heart attack include severe chest pain, profuse sweating, nausea, and pain radiating from the neck down the left arm and leg.

People caring for individuals with heart problems are encouraged to seek medical attention immediately for any symptoms. Heart problems can be fatal. A good cardiologist can diagnose the problem, prescribe medications, and suggest changes in lifestyle habits. It is extremely important to insist that the older person follow the doctor's guidance.

Stroke

A stroke, or cerebrovascular accident, is a disruption of the blood flow to the brain. Strokes are caused by a narrowing of the arteries in the brain (arteriosclerosis), a blood clot (cerebral thrombosis), or a rupture of a blood vessel in the brain. Individuals are affected differently by strokes depending on the location of the problem in the brain. A stroke occurring on one side of the brain affects the other side of the body. Strokes can cause paralysis, slurred speech, and numbness.

People caring for stroke patients should follow the physician's orders. Encourage the patient to address risk factors that contribute to strokes such as high blood pressure, diabetes, smoking, and obesity. Working with therapists can help the patient overcome many of the limitations caused by a stroke. Encourage the patient to practice rehabilitating exercises several times a day to increase muscle strength.

Cancer

Cancer is a descriptive term that refers to diseases caused by the abnormal and uncontrolled division of cells. Tumors, localized masses of new tissue growth, can be malignant and destroy normal, or benign, harmless tissue. Cancer spreads when diseased cells are transported through the blood and lymph system to other parts of the body. A patient is said to be in partial remission when a tumor stops growing or decreases in size; complete remission means that there is no longer any evidence of cancer.

Since many forms of cancer occur more often as people grow older, caregivers of the elderly should be aware of cancer's warning signs.

A cough that does not go away or coughing up blood.

A lump in the breast, change in the shape of the breast, or discharge from the nipple.

Difficulty, increased frequency, and pain while urinating.

Changes in bowel habits or blood in the stool.

Unusual vaginal discharge or bleeding, or pain during intercourse.

A sore that does not heal or a change in a wart or mole.

Caregivers should also make sure that the older person is tested for various forms of cancer as suggested by health care professionals. If the older relative does have cancer, the elder and the caregiver can explore different options for treatment. A second opinion regarding specific treatment is also suggested.

Diabetes

Diabetes is caused by the body's inability to utilize starches and sugars, resulting in abnormally high or low blood sugar levels that can lead to medical emergencies. In diabetics, insulin, the hormone that regulates body sugar levels, is either not available in the proper dosage or is ineffective. Many of the symptoms of diabetes—increased thirst, fatigue, slow healing of cuts, and frequent urination—may go unnoticed. Although diabetes is not curable, it is controllable through diet, exercise, and, in extreme cases, insulin injections.

Caregivers of diabetic patients should monitor the person's diet and exercise habits. In addition, caregivers should examine the older person's skin and feet for redness, blisters, and infections. A podiatrist should be consulted when the older person needs a toenail trimming in order to prevent infection. Skin should be kept clean and dry at all times.

Hypertension

Hypertension, or high blood pressure, is very common among the elderly, particularly African-Americans. A blood pressure reading measures the pressure created against the blood vessels by the flow of blood. For older people, a blood pressure reading higher than 140/90 requires attention. Untreated high blood pressure can lead to heart disease, stroke, or kidney failure.

Caregivers should monitor the older person's blood pressure. They also will want to encourage the patient to eliminate salt from the diet, exercise, and reduce weight. Medication should be taken as directed.

Social Changes

As people age, their social environment changes. Such changes are marked by a decline in social roles and status due to retirement, loss of physical abilities, and loss of friends and family. Older people react differently to these losses. There are three theories that describe how older people adapt to their changing social environment: disengagement, activity, and continuity.

According to the disengagement theory, older people gradually withdraw from social interactions as they turn their attention inward. At the same time, society disengages from the older person. The activity theory suggests that aged people maintain their level of activity by substituting one activity for another, depending on their remaining abilities. The continuity theory implies that commitments are consolidated and time and energy redistributed to the remaining roles as people age.

Retirement

Americans spend more time at work than in any other activity. For most people, work defines who we are and what we contribute to society. And, although employees frequently complain about the frustrations and demands of work, it is through the world of work that people gain a sense of self-esteem. Work represents a major source of income, friendships, and life's challenges.

Like other changes associated with aging, the loss of employment, whether planned or forced, is experienced differently by each individual. Retirement can be viewed as a rite of passage into old age, or it can be identified as a time to relax and enjoy life. For all, retirement represents a major change in how one spends time and the amount of money available. Yet the average American does not plan for retirement or focuses planning mainly on family finances, leaving other important issues unexplored — such as use of leisure time, housing options, health considerations, and family life.

Retirement can affect family life. Spouses may relish the increased time they have to share together, or they may have conflicts or feel there is no time to be alone. Retirement gives aging parents more opportunity to interact with, or interfere in, the lives of adult children or grandchildren.

Caregivers are encouraged to be aware of the older person's adjustment to retirement. As health allows, the caregiver may want to help the older person remain active by encouraging participation in recreational or volunteer opportunities. The caregiver may want to invite the older person on family vacations and other outings. And caregivers may encourage the care receiver to interact more frequently with grandchildren.

Loss of Friends and Spouse

Friendships are more difficult to maintain as people grow older. Friends relocate, some cannot visit due to decreased mobility and illness, while others die. It is not uncommon for a person in the seventh or eighth decade of life to have outlived friends and family members. Loss of friendships can lead to loneliness and depression.

Perhaps the most distressing loss of friendship happens when a spouse dies. The loss of a spouse can be almost unbearable. The surviving spouse may need to alter retirement plans, adjust to a decreased income, learn skills that were once the responsibility of the deceased spouse, and cope with overwhelming grief that can make life seem meaningless.

People caring for someone who has recently lost a spouse need to understand that depression is a normal part of the grieving process. If grieving is prolonged or intense, professional advice may prove useful. Treatment may include psychotherapy, group counseling, or antidepressant medications. According to the book *Parentcare*, some grief reactions should be monitored.

- Mood swings and agitation

- Altered sleeping habits

- Lack of interest in life

- Guilt feelings

- Loss of energy

- Memory and concentration problems

- Changes in appetite

- Thoughts of suicide

Limited Mobility

Limited mobility can be quite distressing for older people. Being able to move around relates to an individual's ability to remain active and connected in the community; it affects socialization, recreation, and employment. Older people can be limited in mobility if they have walking or driving difficulties. In 1988, 19 percent of the elderly living in the community—4.9 million people—had difficulty walking. In addition, poor vision and night blindness prevented many older people from driving.

Caregivers, realizing the importance of social involvement, should encourage care receivers to remain as active as possible. In many cases, older people can venture out into the community with a little assistance. There are many types of equipment designed to assist individuals with mobility. Manual and battery-operated wheelchairs, walkers, crutches, and canes are useful for people who have difficulty walking. In addition, a wheelchair ramp is helpful to those unable to negotiate stairs. And many transportation options may be available in the community.

Mental Changes

Contrary to popular belief, aging does not contribute to drastically decreased mental faculties. Often, factors such as illness, medications, and stress affect mental capabilities more than the aging process itself. Caregivers are cautioned not to attribute signs of mental decline to old age.

Memory

As a person ages, there is a slight decline in memory. Specifically, short-term memory, the ability to recall recent events, diminishes. The capacities for remote memory—that is, memory of events that happened in the past but have been recalled frequently—and old memory—of events that happened in the past but have not been recalled—seem to be retained into advanced age. The ability to remember is related to the intellect and the desire to remember.

Thinking

Thinking is a complex activity in which a person processes information to form opinions, reasoning, and conclusions. Thinking capacity does not change with age, although older individuals may need more time to process information. As with memory, people who have been trained or educated to perform deductions show similar abilities into old age.

Dementia

Dementia is not a disease but rather a complex of symptoms of certain diseases. Dementia is marked by a decline in intellectual functioning that interferes with the ability to complete routine activities. Some forms of dementia are treatable.

Acute Brain Syndrome

An acute brain syndrome is often caused by physical problems such as heart attack, stroke, nutritional deficiencies, dehydration, infections, and brain tumors. The symptoms of acute brain syndrome—confusion, disorientation, and agitation—may mirror those of chronic brain syndrome, except that symptoms appear very suddenly in the acute situation. The most important thing to remember about acute brain syndromes is that they are often treatable and reversible.

Chronic Brain Syndrome

Chronic brain syndromes are caused by arteriosclerosis, low thyroid hormone, pernicious anemia, and other rare diseases.

Symptoms of chronic brain syndrome include loss of intellectual functioning and memory. The initial symptoms are often overlooked, but as the condition progresses over several months and years, the slow decline becomes more obvious. Initially, older people can compensate for short-term memory lapses and a decline in comprehension or thinking. Over time, however, confusion, disorientation, and memory loss become more apparent.

Alzheimer's Disease

Alzheimer's disease (AD) is the most common form of dementia, affecting approximately four million Americans. AD attacks the brain in areas important for memory and intellectual functioning. It is marked by progressive, degenerative decline, which results in impaired memory, thinking, and behavior. Alzheimer's disease is fatal; there is no cure.

SYMPTOMS AND DIAGNOSIS

The symptoms of Alzheimer's disease appear gradually and intensify over time. The patient may begin to have difficulties with memory, intellectual abilities, and language, accompanied by an inability to complete routine activities and a slight disorientation. The prognosis of the disease varies from individual to individual, but it averages 8 years and can last up to 25 years. Eventually, AD patients become unable to care for themselves.

Caregivers should not confuse simple lapses of memory or disorientation with Alzheimer's disease. A diagnosis of AD should be based on complete physical, psychological, and neurological exams. Patients should receive a detailed medical history review, mental status test, comprehensive blood testing, urinalysis, chest X-ray, CAT scan, MRI, and occasionally special studies of the spinal fluid.

A CAT scan (computerized axial tomogram) produces colored images of the brain and is used to detect tumors, loss of brain tissue, and brain disease. An MRI (magnetic resonance imaging) creates a three-dimensional visualization of the brain. Actually, there is no test for identifying AD and it is usually diagnosed after other conditions are ruled out. These exams are used to rule out illnesses that produce symptoms similar to AD such as depression, vascular disorders, infections, drug interaction, or some other physical illness. The only way to confirm a diagnosis of AD is through a brain biopsy immediately after the patient's death.

TIPS FOR CAREGIVERS

Caring for a person with Alzheimer's disease can be challenging and stressful; doing so has been referred to as the 36-hour day. Caregivers are encouraged to contact the Alzheimer's Association at (800) 272-3900 to identify a local chapter. The Alzheimer's Association chapters offer services such as physician referrals, resource materials, support groups, information and referrals, educational seminars, and research updates. In addition, there are a number of strategies that caregivers can employ to deal with difficult behaviors, help the patient cope with the disease, and maintain safety. Several useful suggestions for addressing these areas of concern have been provided by the Alzheimer's Association.

DEALING WITH DIFFICULT BEHAVIOR

Alzheimer's disease affects an older person's personality and often brings about very annoying behaviors. Changes occurring in the brain can cause AD patients to hallucinate, that is, to experience sensory input that does not exist such as seeing or hearing things. They can also be combative, easily agitated, and angry for no apparent reason. Most AD patients wander or may walk away from the house and forget where they live. Incontinence occurs, especially during the latter stages of the disease. The following tips can help caregivers deal with these behaviors:

- Have a physician evaluate the person for physical disorders that cause hallucinations.

- Offer the person reassurance and distraction to turn attention away from hallucinations or frustrating situations.

- Check the environment for noises, objects, glare, or shadows that might be misinterpreted.

- Don't take aggression and anger personally.

- Experiment with things that have a soothing effect such as a stuffed animal, music, or pets.

- Try to avoid situations that cause anxiety for the patient.

- Allow the AD patient to wander within a safe area.

- Encourage physical activity during the day time to decrease wandering at night.

- Prevent the wanderer from getting lost outside the home by using childproof doorknobs, installing an alarm system, or installing a gate around the yard.

- Purchase an identification bracelet or locket.

- Place labels in the patient's clothes that list name, address, and telephone number.

- Alert the neighbors to guide the person home if he or she is found wandering.

- Check with the police department to see if photographs and fingerprints of AD patients can be kept on file.

- Keep a logbook of times when the patient uses the bathroom in order to establish patterns and prevent incontinence.

- Avoid giving an incontinent person diuretics such as coffee, cola, and tea.

- Use a portable commode or urinal during the night.

- Choose easy-to-remove clothing for incontinent patients.

COPING WITH THE DISEASE

People with Alzheimer's disease may experience frustration and depression as they see themselves become increasingly unable to fully participate in life. Caregivers need to understand these feelings and help the patient cope with the changes. Caregivers may find the following coping strategies helpful:

- Treat the patient as a person by using words and touch to communicate slowly and calmly.

- Avoid talking about the person as if he or she were not present.

- Communicate on an adult level, one message at a time, assuming that the person understands what is being said.

- Give praise for simple achievements.

- Tell the person what to expect as you assist with daily care.

- Emphasize what the patient can do and encourage self-care.

- Repeat enjoyable activities.

- Build structure and routine into activities.

- Provide a calm environment at mealtime, and give the person one utensil at a time.

- Use memory aids such as pictures, a clock with large numbers, a calendar, or a daily activity board.

- Prepare the bathroom in advance of bath time.

- Lay out the person's clothes or give a choice of two appropriate outfits to wear.

- Experiment with various clothing fasteners such as Velcro, snaps, and buttons.

MAINTAINING SAFETY

An AD patient may feel anxious and frightened. As the person may not have a normal regard for safety, the caregiver must create a safe environment and monitor the patient's activities. Caregivers may consider some basic safety tips.

- Focus on preventing accidents rather than attempting to teach the patient to adopt safety practices.

- Simplify routines by breaking down procedures into step-by-step processes. Lock away all dangerous substances such as cleaning supplies, medications, and toxic plants.

- Lock away all guns, power tools, knives, and dangerous appliances.

- Remove knobs from the stove in the evening.

- Remove electrical appliances from the bathroom.

- Use safety doorknobs or place locks at the tops or bottoms of doors.

- Use night-lights to illuminate stairs.

- Avoid using high-gloss waxes on furniture and floors.

Minority Aging

In 1990, ethnic minorities composed 10.9 percent of the elderly population. To be old and a member of a minority group is often referred to as double jeopardy, meaning that these elders must deal with the negative consequences of growing older along with the consequences of social and economic discrimination against minorities experienced throughout life. Overall, minority elders in the United States are likely to be less educated, live in substandard housing, and suffer more frequently from poor health and poverty than the nonminority elderly.

Minority elders are a diverse group. Not only are there major racial differences; each ethnic group within a particular race has distinctive characteristics. Ethnicity affects the foods selected, the dialect spoken, life-style and health practices, and religious beliefs. Ethnic culture also affects perceptions of social services, and language differences may limit communication with service providers.

African-Americans

African-American elders represent a little more than 8 percent of the elderly population and make up the fastest growing segment of the African-American population. Older African-Americans are more likely to be divorced, widowed, or separated than whites of the same age. Consequently, many share a home with an adult child rather than a spouse.

About one-third of these elders live in poverty. When compared to whites, today's African-American elders are less educated and are more likely to be sick and disabled. Health, income security, and housing are major concerns for these individuals.

CULTURAL FACTORS

Today's African-American elderly people have lived through decades of intense discrimination and segregation, which may have a direct impact on their current situation and attitudes. As younger adults, they were more likely to be unemployed or under-employed, live in substandard housing, and be denied access to health, social services, and educational systems than their white counterparts. They may remember a time when service organizations intruded into one's personal life, and regulations were designed to discourage the use of services. Many fear that the health system has used African-Americans as guinea pigs during research. Consequently, African-Americans generally look to the family, church, and the community to help them meet their needs.

Caregivers of African-American elders need to understand when cultural factors affect health practices, expectations of help from the family, and resistance to using the formal service system. Understanding these issues will help a caregiver develop strategies to get older people to look beyond the past, culture, and tradition to address their current needs.

For example, it may be unrealistic to expect a 60-year-old African-American woman to immediately stop using salty pork meats while cooking vegetables when she is diagnosed as having high blood pressure. Frequent use of salty pork may be a tradition in her culture. Food does not taste the same without this essential ingredient. The caregiver can start by asking the older person to boil some of the salt off the meat before adding it to vegetables, then slowly show her how to replace the pork by experimenting with herbs and spices.

Another older African-American may resist using social services because of negative experiences. The caregiver may need to guide the person gently through the process, explaining each step.

Asian-Americans

Asian-Americans include a large number of distinct cultural groups. Therefore, one must be cautious in making general statements or constructing categories into which all Asian-Americans might fit. Some 55 percent of this group is concentrated in California, Hawaii, and the state of Washington. Overall, Asian-American elders are likely to be married, with only 19 percent living alone as opposed to 30 percent of the white elderly. Recent immigrants include large numbers of well-educated professionals and, of all minorities, Asian-Americans have the highest percentage of high school graduates. The percentage of Asian-American elderly people living in poverty is similar to that of their white counterparts.

Asian-Americans are a very divergent group, speaking many different languages and holding varied cultural beliefs. Yet, whether Chinese, Japanese, Korean, or Vietnamese, these groups share a traditional respect and sense of obligation toward older family members. The eldest son has traditionally been charged with caring for aging parents. However, depending on the family's degree of acculturation into American society, veneration of Asian-American elders may vary.

Many Asian-Americans resist using formal social services because they expect their families to care for them. In addition, language barriers, negative experiences with the service system, inappropriate services, inaccessible locations, and lack of ethnic programming keep many Asian-Americans from using these services. Many elders in this culture do not make use of formal health services because of cultural and language barriers, a reliance on folk medicine, and a distrust of Western medicine. Often Asian-Americans are unaware that services for the aging exist.

Cultural differences may lead to disagreements between Asian-American care receivers and their caregivers, even when the caregivers are of the same ethnic group. The elderly, particularly those who migrated to this country as adults, may prefer to hold on to old values, customs, and practices, and may not speak English. Some younger Asian-Americans have disregarded traditional customs and practices and may not speak their parents' or grandparents' language. Caregivers who have adopted numerous elements of Western culture may still feel the pull of traditional ethnic values. Understanding this conflict may help caregivers deal with feelings of stress and guilt.

Native Americans

The term *Native American* refers to Indians, Eskimos, and Aleuts, a group in Alaska. About 25 percent of Native Americans live on Indian reservations or in Alaskan native villages, and slightly over half live in rural communities. There are approximately 461 federally recognized Indian tribes and another 200 or more that are not recognized by the government. Tribes speak 250 different languages with several hundred different dialects.

As is true for elderly whites, the majority of elderly male Native Americans are married and the majority of women are widowed. Nearly 12 percent have no formal education and about 22 percent have graduated from high school. About one-third live in poverty. Life expectancy for Native Americans is only 65, eight years less than that of whites. According to *A Portrait of Older Minorities,* Native Americans are at risk of living in substandard housing, poverty, and poor health.

Native Americans are an extremely diverse group. With so many languages and dialects, communicating across cultural groups is difficult. In addition, Native American groups are geographically isolated and most lack adequate public transportation systems. Consequently, many older Native Americans may not participate in social services because they are unaware of them or unable to get to service sites. They may resist medical assistance because of beliefs in traditional ritual healing and a different cultural understanding of disease.

Caregivers of Native Americans must understand and respect the influence of culture on these elders in order to develop positive relationships. Some Native Americans fiercely hold on to traditional customs and resist any suggestion that can be interpreted as abandoning their heritage. Others have little regard for tradition and may be totally assimilated into Western culture. One of the biggest challenges for caregivers is navigating the service system on Indian reservations operated by the U.S. Congress and the Bureau of Indian Affairs.

Hispanics

The term *Hispanic* refers to people of Spanish descent including Mexicans, Puerto Ricans, Cubans, Latin Americans, and others. Approximately 58 percent of today's Hispanic elderly were born in the United States, compared to 88 percent of all elderly.

Hispanics are concentrated in four states—New York, Florida, Texas, and California. And although most older Hispanics speak Spanish, there are several dialects, which may hinder communication among cultural subgroups.

Hispanics are the least educated among minority groups, with 16 percent having no formal education and 19 percent being high school graduates. About 97 percent of Hispanic elderly live in the community, outside of institutions. Approximately one in five older Hispanics live in poverty. And, although older Hispanics are more likely to be in poor health than the elderly in general, they are less likely to have health insurance.

Caregivers of Hispanic elderly people must understand that, if the elder was not born in the United States, he or she may find U.S. laws and practices confusing. Each Hispanic subgroup has a unique history and culture. Traditional Hispanic culture places a high value on the family, and Hispanic elders rely on family members more often than the white and African-American elderly do.

Caregivers of Hispanic elders should consider the importance the care receiver places on the family. Like caregivers of other minority elders, they may need to convince older relatives to accept formal services. In addition, caregivers may need to interpret written materials on services as few have been translated into Spanish.

References

Alzheimer's Association. *Alzheimer's Disease: An Overview*. Chicago: Alzheimer's Association, 1990.

Alzheimer's Association. *Just the Facts*. Chicago: Alzheimer's Association, 1990.

American Association of Retired Persons (AARP), and U.S. Administration on Aging. *A Profile of Older Americans 1990*. Washington, DC: AARP, 1990.

AARP Minority Affairs Initiative. *A Portrait of Older Minorities*. Washington, DC: AARP, 1987.

Bane, Share Decroix, and Burton P. Halpert. *Information for Caregivers of the Elderly: Resource Manual*. Kansas City, MO: University of Missouri-Kansas City, Center on Aging, 1988.

Dartmouth Institute for Better Health, Dartmouth Medical School. *Medical and Health Guide for People over Fifty*. Glenview, IL: Scott, Foresman, 1986.

Horgan, J. "AIDS Researchers Seek to Enroll More Minorities in Clinical Trials." Scientific American 261 (34): 1988.

Jarvik, Lissy, and Gary Small. *Parentcare: A Commonsense Guide to Helping Our Parents*. New York: Crown Publishers, 1988.

New York State Office for the Aging. *Caregivers Practical Help*. Buffalo, NY: New York State Department on Aging, 1987.

U.S. Department of Health and Human Services, Agency for Health Care Policy and Research. *Use of Home and Community Services by Persons Age 65 and Older with Functional Difficulties*. Research Finding 5, DHHS publication no. 90-3466. Washington, DC: U.S. Department of Health and Human Services, September 1990.

Chapter 3

Informal and Formal Supports

Introduction

Most older people prefer to remain in familiar surroundings. The home represents a sense of comfort, familiarity, and independence. There are numerous options for providing the elderly with the assistance they need in order to achieve the maximum independence in the least restrictive environment.

Supports for the elderly can be categorized as informal and formal. Informal supports are people who help the elder and may include family, friends, neighbors, church or synagogue members, and others who are willing to provide assistance, often at no cost. The term *formal support* refers to services offered by private or public organizations and agencies whose mission includes serving the elderly. Both informal and formal supports are available to assist caregivers as well as care receivers.

The availability of supports varies, depending on the presence and willingness of the informal network and the limitations of community resources. For example, many elderly people do not have relatives living nearby, or they may have outlived their families, friends, and neighbors. In other cases, for numerous reasons, family and friends may be unwilling or unable to provide assistance.

Access to formal services is restricted by the lack of knowledge about services, limited finances, exclusive program requirements, and long waiting lists. For example, in small rural communities, consumers often experience difficulty in gaining access to services because of the vast geographic distances between individuals and the lack of adequate public transportation. In large metropolitan areas, there are long waiting lists for some programs or the fees for services might be prohibitive.

Nonetheless, informal and formal supports are vital to the care of older adults. Such supports assure that aging persons receive the types of care needed at the frequency required. They also relieve some of the stress, both physical and emotional, experienced by the caregiver. Through appropriate use of available resources, older people can prevent premature institutionalization.

This chapter addresses informal and formal supports. It identifies sources of informal support and barriers to the use of it, reviews community-based and in-home services, and provides tips for dealing with the social service system.

Informal Supports

Case Study

Mrs. Jones is a 73-year-old woman who suffers from severe arthritis and asthma. On many days she is unable to dress herself or prepare meals. She leaves her home only for doctor's appointments.

Mrs. Jones lives with her 53-year-old single daughter, Linda, who is employed full-time outside the home. Mrs. Jones also has two sons, Joe and Sam. Joe visits with his mother two to three times per week and gives her expensive presents on her birthday and at Christmas. Sam seldom visits or calls because his job is very demanding, and he prefers spending his free time with his two teenage sons.

Linda worries about her mother during the day while she is at work, yet she cannot call home frequently because her supervisor is not understanding. Caring for her mother is beginning to affect Linda financially and physically. She strained her back a month ago transferring her mother from the commode to the wheelchair. She spends approximately $120 per month on her mother's medication and the incontinent pads she must wear at night. Linda resents her brothers for not helping.

Joe works approximately ten hours per day. He is more than willing to assist his mother but does not know how he can help. His mother cannot visit him because there are two flights of stairs leading to his apartment. At times, he feels sorry for Linda because she looks so tired and worn down. Yet, when he asks how things are going, Linda always responds, "Just fine." He does not offer to help because he thinks Linda will not accept his assistance.

Sam is so engrossed in his career and family that he does not even recognize that Linda and his mother need help. He does not visit often because he finds it difficult to watch his mother deteriorate. Sam and Linda have never gotten along well, and he feels uncomfortable talking to her. Sam believes that Linda will call him if she needs anything.

The case of the Jones family highlights the frustrations experienced by many caregivers who give care for a prolonged period of time without support from other family members. It also reflects typical family dynamics. Linda feels overburdened but does not ask her brothers for help; Joe is willing to provide assistance but is unsure of how to approach Linda; and Sam is not even aware that assistance is needed and has difficulty dealing with the fact that his mother is aging. Consequently, due to a lack of communication, each sibling must deal with difficult emotions alone.

In most caregiving situations, one person provides most of the care needed by the older person. This person is commonly referred to as the primary caregiver. Primary caregivers often feel alone and isolated. They feel no one is available to assist with physical and financial burdens and that no one will listen and understand their concerns.

On the other hand, many primary caregivers believe they are the only people who can give quality care. And they feel guilty if someone else does "their job." Many worry if they are not always available to make sure the older person's needs are being met satisfactorily. They experience mixed emotions about providing care and feel ashamed of having so-called negative emotions.

Caregivers must understand that it is appropriate to ask for help and that the conflicting emotions experienced are normal. In most cases, it is virtually impossible for one person to provide constant care without feeling emotional and physical exhaustion. Accepting assistance is healthy. Support from others will prolong the caregiver's ability to give care and help assure that the older person receives adequate care. In addition, accepting help will allow the caregiver time to focus on the positive aspects of the relationship with the care receiver.

Typically, others besides the primary caregiver are deeply concerned about the welfare of the older person. These individuals may have very loving feelings toward the older person and want to help in any way possible. Sometimes they do not come forward to offer a specific form of help because they are unsure about what is needed or how the primary caregiver will respond to their offer of assistance.

It is equally important for the care receiver to realize that the primary caregiver cannot bear this burden alone. Some older people have a difficult time understanding that their caregiver needs help with care-related tasks, and they may resist the idea of someone else giving care. Others equate the need for outside assistance with a lack of affection on the part of the caregiver. Many older people refuse to accept assistance from others because they are ashamed to let others know about their limitations or they do not want strangers in the house.

When possible, the older person and the caregiver should discuss the need for outside help, allowing the older person to raise concerns. Perhaps some of these objections are valid and can serve as a point of negotiation. For example, an older man may not want a female church member to assist him with bathing or grooming, but he might be delighted to have her prepare and share meals with him.

In some instances, the older person is unwilling to compromise and refuses to cooperate. In this case, the caregiver must remember that receiving help is a necessity and examine ways to get support in the least intrusive manner. For example, if the older person refuses to allow anyone in the home to assist with household chores, the caregiver could arrange to have someone come in while the older person is out of the home. Or the caregiver could ask the person providing help to take the dirty laundry home or assist with yard work.

Identifying Needs

The Checklist of Concerns/Resources for Caregivers, shown in Figure 1, is useful for identifying areas where assistance is needed. Other needs can be added to the checklist. Once the older person and the caregiver have agreed on areas where assistance would be useful, they can begin matching people from the informal network list with areas of need.

If you or your relative agrees with one of the following statements, place a "1" in the space provided to the left. These are your primary concerns. Place a "2" in the space if you think the statement may be applicable in the future. These are your secondary concerns. The information contained in the brackets following each statement identifies the type of assistance needed.

My older relative:

_____ really needs to get out and do something (Socialization or Volunteering).

_____ can do light housecleaning but needs assistance with heavy tasks (Chore Services).

_____ has some legal matters that needs attention (Legal).

_____ is grieving over the death of a loved one (Bereavement Support).

_____ cannot drive or use public transportation, and taxicabs are too expensive (Transportation).

_____ is unable to remain in his or her present housing (Housing).

_____ needs help with food preparation, housekeeping, or laundry (Homemaker Services).

_____ needs assistance with personal care (Home-Health or Personal Care Aide).

_____ doesn't eat right (Nutrition).

_____ cannot be left alone during the day (Friendly Visitors or Intermediate Care Facility).

_____ needs special services for physical limitations and impairments (Handicapped Services).

_____ has very high health care costs (Medical Insurance Options).

_____ is depressed, suspicious, or angry all the time, or just sits (Complete Geriatric Evaluation).

_____ really needs 24-hour supervision even though he or she fights it (Private Nurse or Nursing Home).

_____ has a terminal illness and wants to die at home (Hospice).

Sometimes I feel:

_____ overwhelmed; I have so many unanswered questions about aging and services for the elderly (Information and Referral or Care Management).

_____ I honestly need to share my feelings with someone who would understand (Counseling or Support Group).

_____ other family members are not helping enough (Family Meeting).

_____ my caregiving responsibilities are negatively affecting my work, personal life, and health (Physical Exam, Stress Management, and Complete Medical Evaluation).

Figure 1   Checklist of Concerns/Resources for Caregivers (This checklist was adapted from the AARP's Checklist of Concerns/Resources for Caregivers. Courtesy of AARP.)

Identifying Sources of Informal Supports

Once the older person and the caregiver agree that outside assistance is needed, they can make a list of the elements in their informal network—all the people who might be interested in helping. Start with family, friends, and neighbors. Remember to include children and other older relatives. At this point, do not make any judgments about each person's willingness or abilities; simply add all the names to the list.

Next, examine the organizations in which the aging person has been involved. These include churches and synagogues, service organizations, unions, charities, retiree clubs, and social groups. Some of these groups provide services to seniors, or individual members may be able to provide companionship or emergency assistance in addition to hands-on support.

After the informal network list is complete, review the relationship each person listed has with the older person. Past disagreements and bitterness may eliminate several people from the list. It is best to exclude individuals who would cause more stress and strain than actual assistance.

It is important to keep in mind that, although a person may seem perfectly suited to provide a particular service, that person may be unwilling or unable to do so. Caregivers need to negotiate with people who agree to provide support, remaining aware that these people also have other responsibilities and demands. The most important concern is to assure that as many needs as possible are being met, bearing in mind the need for emergency support when a helper is unable to complete an assignment.

Tips for Maintaining an Ongoing Informal Support System

Ask for help   Asking others for help can be difficult, although there are usually many people who are willing to assist. Caregivers may resist asking for help because they feel that interested people should offer assistance without being asked.

There are many reasons why potential helpers do not take the initiative to provide care. People hesitate to offer help when they do not feel their assistance is needed or wanted. Perhaps they do not want to appear intrusive or fear that they cannot measure up to the standards set by the caregiver. Realizing these facts, you may have to take the first step in securing assistance from the informal network. When asking for help, specify what needs to be done, schedule helpers appropriately, and express appreciation.

Be specific　In order to feel useful and successful, helpers need to know exactly what is expected of them. Caregivers should specify exactly what is to be done; how it is to be done, if necessary; and when it is to be done and why. This provides a context for the assistance to be delivered and helps volunteers understand the importance of tasks being performed. However, do not to sound too restrictive in specifying instructions for a task; instead, provide guidance and allow various approaches to getting a particular job done.

Schedule　It is very important to schedule informal supports so that all needs are met and care is available when needed. Avoid scheduling several people for the same time period. The goal is to construct a complementary system of support. If volunteers believe their assistance is not needed, they may discontinue providing support. Similarly, avoid overburdening one person; instead, distribute the work load evenly.

You may find it helpful to keep track of informal supports by developing a monthly calendar of what others have agreed to do and when support will be provided. It may be useful to share a copy of the calendar with people providing help. Initially, until everyone is comfortable with referring to the calendar, you may need to call helpers a couple of days in advance to remind them of a particular commitment. In emergency situations, simply contact the people whose names are recorded on the informal support list as being able to provide emergency assistance.

Show appreciation　Remember the importance of showing appreciation for the assistance received. Everyone enjoys feeling appreciated. It is quite natural to express gratitude when someone agrees to help. Sometimes, however, assistance goes unrecognized over a long period of time and the helper can feel taken for granted. Small tokens of appreciation such as thank-you cards, home-cooked dinners, pictures of the helper with the older person, and verbal praise in the presence of others can help a volunteer sustain interest in providing care.

Formal Supports

The term *formal supports* refers to social services designed to meet the needs of the elderly and the people who assist them. Formal services include those based in the community such as nutrition sites, adult day-care centers, and senior transportation services. They also include home-based services such as meals-on-wheels, home-health care, and chore services. In recent years, the formal service system, like the informal system, has been strained by the dramatic increase in the elderly population, the increased complexity of their needs, inflation, and changes in government financing of services.

The availability of specific services varies from community to community. More services may be available in large metropolitan areas than in smaller communities or rural areas. Even when services are available, many consumers are not aware of them. And caregivers may have difficulty accessing services if the system is fragmented with multiple providers, and various programs have different eligibility criteria and various payment methods. Such incongruity causes consumers to shy away from formal services. In fact, according to *A National Survey of Caregivers* conducted for American Association of Retired Persons (AARP) in 1988, 22 percent of caregivers do not use formal services at all.

Caregivers fail to use services for many of the same reasons that they resist using informal supports. However, there may be additional elements of concern when one must deal with a bureaucracy. The application process for some programs requires that older people share personal information with strangers. Services may not be conveniently located. And, in the case of in-home services, the older person must allow a stranger in the home. Many caregivers feel guilty about using services, and many older people resist the idea of accepting what they see as charity.

Despite the barriers and the ambiguous feelings associated with service use, formal services can add to the quality of life for most older people and caregivers. The appropriate services can help older people avoid unnecessary institutionalization.

FACTS

• In 1987, a total of 4.6 million elderly people with functional difficulties received no formal services, compared to 2.3 million who used at least one service.

• Functional status and living arrangements strongly relate to the use of formal services by older people. The greater the functional limitation, the more likely an older person will use services. Similarly, people who live alone are about twice as likely to use services as those who live with another person.

• Some 65 percent of caregivers use at least one social service to help them perform caregiving-related activities.

• Few caregivers make use of services created specifically to provide support to them, such as educational seminars (used by 17 percent of caregivers), respite care (10 percent), and support groups (12 percent).

The Aging Network

The Older Americans Act (OAA) was enacted in 1965 "to provide assistance in the development of new or improved programs to help older persons." The OAA created a federal office to oversee implementation of the act, the Administration on Aging (AoA). Each state also has an agency designated as the State Unit on Aging (SUA), which is charged with developing and administering a state plan on aging that reflects national objectives established by the AoA. The SUAs also serve as a state focal point for all issues concerning older people.

Each state is comprised of several planning and service areas. Within each planning and service area, an Area Agency on Aging (AAA) establishes a comprehensive and coordinated system of service delivery. There are approximately 670 AAAs in the United States. The AAAs contract with local organizations for the provision of services. In many instances, AAAs offer direct services in order to assure that citizens have access to appropriate programs. In addition, AAAs are mandated to offer information regarding services available to older people living in their jurisdictions.

The aging network consists of these federal, state, and local agencies that are devoted exclusively to developing, coordinating, and monitoring resources and services funded by funds from the OAA. This structure was developed to assure that Americans have access to a systematic, planned array of services.

Community-Based Services

Caregivers and older citizens can take advantage of a number of services in the community in order to improve their quality of life and prevent unnecessary institutionalization. Again, availability of specific services varies by community.

FACTS

- About 2.7 million people a year participate in congregate meals programs.

- There are approximately 2,100 adult day-care centers in the United States serving approximately 50,000 frail elderly people.

- In 1986, approximately 1.2 million older people used special transportation services.

- In 1989, the National Council on Aging identified 750 caregiver support groups across the country. The Alzheimer's Association, however, reports sponsoring approximately 1,600 support groups.

CONGREGATE MEALS

Nutritionally balanced meals offered in a group setting are referred to as congregate meals. These programs, typically offered at noon several days a week, provide one-third of an individual's daily nutritional requirement. Perhaps just as important, congregate meal programs allow isolated elderly people the opportunity to socialize with peers. Many programs also offer recreational activities and health screenings. Some programs are linked to senior transportation services to accommodate older people who do not drive or use public transportation.

These services contribute greatly to the overall health of the elderly. Older people with moderate to severe physical or mental limitations may find congregate meals unsuitable, as most participants are fairly active and the programs are not staffed to provide physical assistance or monitoring. People who are isolated and have trouble shopping for groceries or preparing meals benefit the most. Meals are normally low in fat and sodium. Some programs are able to accommodate other dietary restrictions if given prior notice.

Congregate meals are frequently served at senior centers, churches, and community centers. Meals are usually offered free or at a low cost. Donations of 50 cents to $3 may be encouraged. Many programs require reservations.

ADULT DAY CARE

Adult day-care centers generally operate during normal business hours, although some are open from 7 A.M. to 6 P.M. Adult day-care centers provide a safe, supportive, and therapeutic setting for elderly people with physical or mental disabilities or both. Services available at day-care centers vary, but most offer an array of health, social, and support services, depending on the staff. Participants usually receive a hot lunch and a snack. Sometimes transportation is provided.

There are three models of adult day care, although many centers combine models. The first is the medical model, which emphasizes health and rehabilitative services such as nursing and occupational, speech, and physical therapies. These centers employ or contract for nursing staff and therapists and are frequently operated by hospitals and nursing homes. Participants attending medical-model centers often have significant functional limitations.

The second model is referred to as social and emphasizes recreation, socialization, and assistance with activities of daily living. Social-model centers employ or contract for social workers and recreational staff and are frequently operated by senior centers and community and family service agencies. Participants are not very frail and need minimal assistance and supervision.

The final model, representing 5 to 7 percent of centers, serves only individuals with cognitive impairments such as Alzheimer's disease patients. These centers have a lower staff-client ratio and focus on reality orientation, safety, and therapeutic stimulation and exercise. Staff members at these centers are trained to deal with dementia.

Adult day care alleviates isolation for impaired elderly individuals. It allows them an opportunity to socialize with peers and participate in interesting activities. For caregivers, adult day-care centers provide respite (temporary relief from caregiving). Many caregivers, particularly employed people, feel less stressed during the day when the aging person is in a supportive, supervised environment.

Before admitting a person into the program, the adult day-care center staff typically conducts an assessment to assure that the individual is appropriate for the center. Adult day-care centers serve older people with chronic illnesses, functional limitations, and disabilities. Some centers will not accept a person who is incontinent, dangerous, extremely disruptive, or unable to walk alone or with an assistive device. If the person is accepted, an individualized plan of care is developed. Centers usually require that patients attend on a regular basis, at least twice a week.

Caregivers or care receivers frequently pay day-care fees in advance. In 1989, fees for adult day-care centers averaged $30 to $40 per day. Fees may be adjusted according to a sliding scale, based on the ability to pay. Medicaid, a state-administered health insurance program for low-income or medically needy people, pays for adult day care in some states. Medicare, the federal health insurance program for people 65 and older, reimburses consumers for skilled medical services rendered at the center if ordered by a physician. Some long-term care insurance policies also cover the costs of adult day care.

CAREGIVER SUPPORT GROUPS

Caregiver support groups have existed for a little more than ten years. These groups allow people caring for the elderly to share coping strategies and practical information. Caregivers are also able to express their emotions in a supportive, nonjudgmental environment. Many support groups meet biweekly or monthly during the evening, although some meet during the day or on weekends. Meetings are held at such sites as libraries, hospitals, agency offices, senior centers, and adult day-care facilities. The meetings are structured to allow participants the opportunity to express their concerns and learn about practical skills and resources from community experts. Group leaders are professionals or knowledgeable caregivers.

Support groups are an invaluable resource for caregivers. People undergoing the same experience can frequently share feelings that are difficult to discuss with family members and friends. Participants know that other group members are dealing with similar feelings and difficulties and may have valuable solutions to offer. Through support groups, caregivers learn about community resources and effective coping skills, and they may develop lasting friendships.

Organizations such as the Alzheimer's Association, Area Agencies on Aging, hospitals, churches, social services, and aging services sponsor caregiver support groups. Many other informal groups are not associated with an organization or service. About half of caregiver support groups are open to all caregivers. The other groups were organized to meet the needs of a particular type of caregiver such as people caring for Alzheimer's disease patients or adult children of aging parents. In most groups, there is no charge for participating.

RESPITE CARE

Respite care services allow caregivers time away from caregiving demands to rest, participate in recreational activities, run errands, or simply visit with friends. Respite care can help prevent caregiver burnout. It allows a person to step away from a stress-ful situation for a short break. Caregivers who use respite ser-vices report that they have more emotional and physical stamina as a result.

Community-based respite care is available on a limited basis through hospitals, personal care homes, and nursing homes. Many adult day-care services also serve as respite sites. With community-based programs, the older person is taken out of the home for a couple hours per day. Although not widely avail-able yet, a few programs provide respite care for a weekend, an entire week, or up to one month. Fees can vary greatly. Services are free, based on a sliding fee scale, or priced by the hour or day. In some states, Medicaid pays for respite care.

TRANSPORTATION

Special transportation services for seniors are available in most communities with a number of options provided. Transit author-ities are required to offer discount fares to seniors. Churches, taxis, senior housing complexes, and private transportation com-panies also offer special transportation for older citizens. Many of these services can accommodate wheelchair-using passengers. Some services offer transportation for any purpose, responding on demand, while others assist only with special needs such as doctor's appointments or grocery shopping. Some services oper-ate on a regular schedule and some require reservations. In some communities, paid or volunteer escorts are available to accom-pany elderly people on trips.

Senior transportation is a liberator for elderly people who can no longer drive or who have difficulty walking long distances. Without transportation, seniors are denied access to the commu-nity. Transportation programs, coupled with escort services, lessen the demand on the caregiver to transport the older person on all trips. This is especially comforting to employed caregivers who have to take time away from work to transport the senior to daytime appointments.

Fees for transportation services vary by community and type of provider. For example, public transportation may be 50 per-cent less expensive for the elderly, some transportation services for the elderly and handicapped are free, and some private transportation companies charge up to $35 per trip. In some cases, people eligible for Medicaid receive reimbursement for rides to medical facilities. Medicare reimburses transportation costs for homebound, nonambulatory people for emergency medical purposes.

Home-Based Services

Social services delivered to an individual's home include home-health services, meals, visitor programs, and respite care. Designed to maximize independence for older people who need support and supervision, home-based services are growing in number and complexity.

FACTS

- In 1987, 19.7 percent of people 65 and older with functional disabilities used professional home-care or homemaker services. Homemakers provided almost half of the home-care services received.

- Approximately 6.1 percent of functionally limited elders received home-delivered meals in 1987.

- Approximately 30 companies nationwide market personal emergency response systems. About 350,000 people subscribe to these services.

- According to the AARP, the national average cost of home care exceeds $60 per visit.

HOMEMAKER OR CHORE SERVICES

Homemakers assist the elderly with light housekeeping tasks such as housecleaning, preparing meals, laundry, ironing, and grocery shopping. Chore services include heavy tasks like mowing the lawn, minor household repairs, washing windows, and shoveling snow. Some homemaker services also assist with personal care. The people actually providing the care are called homemaker's aides and personal care aides. Agencies offering homemaker services may be private and nonprofit home-health companies, religious groups, or family service organizations.

Many consumers hire their own homemakers. Word of mouth and advertising in the newspaper are good ways to identify potential employees. Having a clear idea of the kinds of help they need, the type of person they want to hire, and the fees they are willing to pay, gives consumers a good basis for screening out inappropriate applicants.

During the interview, the potential caregiver and the older person should discuss issues such as responsibilities, hours, wages, and benefits. The care receiver should provide a written summary so that all people have a clear understanding of the job. Employers can ask about the applicant's background, training, and experience. The caregiver should check references of all candidates being considered for employment.

If a homemaker is hired directly by a consumer without going through an agency, several legal requirements and benefits must be met. The employer must apply for an employer identification number by completing the IRS form SS-4. Consumers are responsible for holding and matching Social Security payments, federal and state unemployment taxes, and workmen's compensation if required by the state. Additionally, the homemaker may desire to have state and federal income taxes withheld.

IRS form 942, "Employer's Quarterly Tax Return for Household Employees," details exactly how to make Social Security and income tax payments, and IRS form 940 details how to make unemployment payments. Caregivers should contact the local tax office for guidelines on state unemployment taxes and workmen's compensation coverage. Caregivers can also check on liability insurance to cover in-home workers. This can sometimes be handled through homeowner's insurance policies.

Fees for homemaker services are usually billed by the hour or by the visit, and they vary greatly among communities. On average, agencies pay homemakers $5.65 per hour. The cost of private homemaker services are seldom reimbursed by insurance carriers. In some states, Medicaid reimburses the cost of homemakers.

HOME-HEALTH CARE

Home-health care refers to health services brought into the home and includes diagnostic, treatment, rehabilitative, and supportive services. In identifying the services a patient needs in the home, an interdisciplinary team of professionals, in consultation with the care receiver's primary care physician, develops an individualized plan of care. Care plans can include skilled and personal care services and durable medical equipment such as wheelchairs, hospital beds, and dialysis machines.

Skilled medical services are delivered by nursing professionals and therapists. Nursing care includes administering medications, changing sterile dressings, and catheter care. Physical therapists perform therapeutic exercises; speech therapists help patients practice language skills; and occupational therapists help individuals complete daily activities and provide assistive devices, if necessary. These professionals also instruct the patient and family members on basic home-care techniques.

Trained paraprofessionals known as home-health aides or personal care attendants can perform personal care, bathing, dressing, grooming, feeding, meal preparation, and laundry. Many home-health agencies provide consumers with durable medical equipment, namely wheelchairs, walkers, hospital beds, oxygen equipment, and testing or monitoring equipment. Consumers can purchase equipment or arrange for rentals.

Home-health care services are beneficial to people recuperating at home, the chronically ill or disabled, and people needing technologically advanced treatment. Without home-health care, many of these individuals would be unable to remain in their homes.

According to the National Association for Home Care, there are some 12,500 home-health agencies in this country. The numerous providers of home-health care include the Visiting Nurse Association, private nonprofit and for-profit companies, hospitals, corporations, city and county health departments, and hospice organizations.

Most states require home-health agencies to be licensed, but licensing requirements differ from state to state. In some states, only Medicare-certified agencies are licensed; in other states, agencies that provide personal care must apply for a license. A license is given when the organization adheres to minimal business and safety standards of a given jurisdiction.

If an agency meets the standards of care set by Medicare, it may qualify as a Medicare-certified provider and receive payment for Medicare-covered services. As of September 1990, there were 5,721 Medicare-certified home-health providers.

In addition, recent legislation known as the Omnibus Budget Reconciliation Act of 1987 (OBRA) mandates that Medicare-certified organizations offer expanded consumer protection. In 1991, the legislation required that agencies

- Employ only trained and certified home-health aides
- Inform consumers of their rights such as confidentiality of medical records
- Offer a written grievance process
- Let consumers participate in care planning
- Give receivers advance notice of changes in care
- Provide users with estimates of the amount of charges that will be covered by Medicare

Each state also must operate a toll-free home-health telephone hotline and an investigative unit to provide information about and receive complaints regarding certified agencies. Chapter 8 contains a list of Medicare home-health hotlines.

An accredited service is an organization that has voluntarily met the stringent standards developed by the accrediting organization. Accrediting organizations include the Joint Commission on the Accreditation of Healthcare Organizations, the Foundation for Hospice and Home Care, and the National League for Nursing.

Home-health care agencies charge different rates for different services. Fees vary greatly among agencies. Marion Merrill Dow Inc., a pharmaceutical company, reports that the average per-visit rates charged for home-care services in 1990 were $85 for social work, $72 for nursing services, $73 for physical therapy, and $42 for home-health aides. Some agencies offer a sliding scale. Fees for services on evenings and weekends are sometimes higher than on weekdays.

Medicare reimburses care receivers for nursing services and occupational, speech, or physical therapy, provided that the following requirements are met:

- The consumer is enrolled in either Medicare Part A (hospital insurance) or Part B (medical insurance).

- The individual is confined to the home, that is, the person needs assistance to leave the home or leaving the home is contradictory to medical advice.

- Care is medically reasonable and necessary, as determined by a physician.

- Part-time or intermittent care is needed. Part-time is defined as less than eight hours per day. Intermittent is defined as eight hours a day for fewer than seven days a week, or eight hours a day for seven days a week for up to 38 consecutive days.

If consumers qualify for home-health reimbursement under Medicare, they may also be eligible for reimbursement for part-time or intermittent home-health aides, medical social services, medical supplies, and medical equipment. Medicare pays 100 percent of approved home-care charges and 80 percent of approved charges for durable medical equipment.

Medicaid covers home-care services in some states. Eligible consumers must meet monthly income and asset limits, which vary from state to state. States can provide home-health services through Medicaid by offering optional long-term care services or obtaining a wavier to offer home- and community-based services to people at risk of institutionalization. Medicaid waiver programs are offered by 41 states.

Medicaid pays the entire cost of home-health care for eligible consumers. Consumers should make sure in advance that the agency delivering the services accepts Medicaid. Some agencies do not participate in the Medicaid program because the reimbursement rate is low.

CARE MANAGEMENT

Care or case management is becoming an important support for elderly individuals with multiple problems. This service helps older people and their caregivers identify their needs, coordinate services, and monitor the care being provided. After an assessment is completed, a thorough review of the informal support system, medical condition, functional limitations, and financial resources is made, and an individualized care plan is developed. A care plan spells out established goals, the services needed, when services will be delivered and by whom, and how services will be purchased. Some care management programs assist clients with the application process for services by completing necessary paperwork. Care managers monitor the client's progress and revise the plan of care as needed.

Care management services are most appropriate for individuals with multiple needs or people without an informal network of support. In many communities, there is no central source of information on services available. As a result, older people and their caregivers are often overwhelmed and frustrated as they attempt to negotiate the system, especially if the caregiver lives in a different city. Care managers help their clients sort through the complicated system of health and social services, and find and coordinate services that meet their particular situations.

Care management services are offered by Area Agencies on Aging, state health departments, and social service organizations. Private sources of care management services include hospitals, long-term care insurance carriers, and private geriatric care managers. In some states, Medicaid picks up the cost of these services. Public agencies may offer the service free or on a sliding scale basis. Private geriatric care managers typically charge $100 to $300 for the initial assessment and $50 to $150 per hour thereafter.

MEALS PROGRAMS

Home-delivered meals programs provide nutritionally balanced meals to elderly people who cannot prepare food unassisted. These programs are frequently referred to as meals-on-wheels. Generally, a hot meal is delivered at noontime, five days per week. However, some programs also deliver a cold evening meal that simply needs to be heated and meals on the weekends.

Home-delivered meals programs are offered through the local department on aging, religious organizations, or community service agencies. Volunteers frequently deliver the meals. Most meals-on-wheels programs are free or reasonably priced.

FRIENDLY VISITORS

Friendly visitors or senior companions provide social interaction for the homebound elderly. Typically, volunteers visit the elderly person at regularly scheduled times. Volunteers are trained to detect potential problems and report them to the program staff. The visitor's primary function is to provide companionship, through talking, reading letters or books to the elderly person, reminiscing, or playing games. Most volunteers do not perform household tasks.

Friendly visitor programs are frequently run by religious organizations, volunteer organizations, and public agencies. Normally, there is no charge for companions.

TELEPHONE REASSURANCE

Telephone reassurance programs, like friendly visitor services, provide homebound elderly people with frequent contact with the outside world. Volunteers telephone the elderly person at specified times, usually on a daily basis. They provide conversation and can also remind the older person to take medication or to eat. If the older person does not answer the telephone, volunteers are trained to contact the staff coordinator so that relatives can be alerted. Programs are run by religious and voluntary organizations and public agencies. The majority of programs are provided at no cost.

IN-HOME RESPITE

Respite care services allow caregivers time away from caregiving demands to rest, participate in recreational activities, run errands, or simply visit friends. Respite workers come into the home on a prearranged basis, typically from two to eight hours per day. In some instances, respite workers function similarly to friendly visitors in addition to monitoring the well-being of the senior. In other instances, respite workers function like homemakers and prepare meals and assist with personal care.

Respite care is available on a limited basis through aging departments and service organizations. In-home respite services cost between $4 and $10 per hour, although many services are free or based on a sliding scale. Some states provide respite care services through the Medicaid waiver program.

PERSONAL EMERGENCY RESPONSE SYSTEM

Personal emergency response systems (PERS) allow older people to signal for help 24 hours per day, in case of an emergency, by pressing a small transmitter or a portable help button. When the transmitter is depressed, preselected emergency telephone numbers are dialed through a console connected to the telephone. Unfortunately, there is no way to verify whether the distress message is received.

Some systems automatically dial a control center that instantly locates the older person's file, which contains pertinent information including the names and telephone numbers of people to be contacted in case of an emergency. With some systems, the console is a two-way speaker phone that allows the staff in the center to communicate with the older person and attempt to ascertain the nature of the problem before signaling for emergency assistance.

AARP notes that there are approximately 30 national companies marketing PERS. A larger number of local companies have recently started offering the service. Most services are associated with medical centers or senior housing facilities. The number of providers is expected to increase rapidly over the next five to ten years.

PERS give older people and their caregivers an added sense of security. Many older people are afraid of falling or becoming ill when no one is around. This form of support is appropriate for frail individuals who live alone.

Consumers can purchase, lease, or rent PERS. Consumers will spend anywhere from $200 to more than $1,000 to purchase a system. Leasing and rental fees vary, depending on the equipment selected. In addition, users are typically required to pay a monthly monitoring fee which averaged $10 to $45 in 1989. There are few avenues for reimbursement for personal emergency response systems, although hospitals may offer reduced rates for low-income people.

Accessing the Formal System

In most large metropolitan areas, many services are available to assist older people and caregivers. Small communities and rural areas tend to have fewer services. Yet availability does not always translate into accessibility. Navigating the service maze can be exhausting and frustrating. Overall, the service system is fragmented with multiple providers that do not coordinate their activities well. Different services use different eligibility criteria and funding mechanisms. Consequently, the average caregiver is often confused.

CASE STUDY

Jessica Sims is returning to work in one week after quitting her job two years ago to care for her grandmother. Jessica has been told by friends that service organizations will care for her grandmother while she is at work. Jessica and her grandmother have decided to find a service that will help with bathing, dressing, and preparing lunch.

Jessica begins her quest to locate services with the telephone book. She calls her local department on aging. She tells the receptionist that she needs someone to prepare a hot lunch for her grandmother and is immediately put on hold. After three minutes, the receptionist gives her numbers for three meals-on-wheels programs. When Jessica calls the first, the line is busy. She calls the second and is told she needs to call the first number because that agency serves her area. After calling the first program five times, she gets through. She arranges for meals and asks if someone can help her grandmother get bathed and dressed during the morning. She is told to call the department on aging.

She calls the department on aging and is disconnected while being transferred. After calling back, she is transferred to the social worker's line and is told that the social worker is on a home visit. The next day, the social worker calls back and tells her to call XYZ community service agency, which serves her area. She calls XYZ community agency and is told to call ABC home-health care agency and to request a home-health aide. She calls ABC home-health care agency and is told that a case manager will need to complete an assessment before the service can begin. She is told that the earliest possible date for an assessment would be on her third day of work.

The next day, Jessica's new employer telephones to say that he looks forward to her attending training next week. Jessica immediately calls ABC home-health care agency to reschedule the assessment. She cannot remember the name of the person who scheduled the appointment. After being transferred and put on hold, Jessica decides that she would rather bathe and groom her grandmother before she leaves for work than deal with social services.

This scenario is not intended to suggest that all interactions with service agencies are negative. It highlights areas in which the consumer could have been better prepared. The following suggestions can help consumers prepare to deal with service providers.

MAKING THE SYSTEM WORK FOR YOU

Plan Ahead   Most people seek formal services as a last resort, often during a crisis. At such a time, the consumer may be unable to review options or plan effectively. Although the future condition of an older relative is unpredictable, there are often signs of impending disability or other issues of concern. Caregivers should be aware of subtle signs that the older person is experiencing difficulties and think of how those difficulties will affect the elder's ability to perform various activities of self-care.

Know What Is Needed   Before calling an agency, caregivers should identify exactly what they need. Caregivers should think in terms of how often assistance will be needed and when assistance is required. And future needs should be anticipated. The Checklist of Concerns/Resources for Caregivers, Figure 1, is a useful tool for identifying needs. A social worker or a case manager also may provide helpful insights. If possible, consumers will want to apply the terminology used by people working in the field of aging to ensure smooth communications.

Identify Several Service Providers   Knowing where to begin looking for help is challenging. A good place to start is the local department on aging or a local senior center. Another good source of information is the telephone directory. In the government section, look under Aging, Senior Citizens, or Human Services. In the yellow pages, look under a heading that describes the service needed. Many communities have information and referral services to help consumers identify needed services. Another good source of information is the local United Way agency. Trusted individuals such as doctors, nurses, family members, friends, and neighbors may have useful leads.

Begin A File   Use a small book to record information gathered about each agency that addresses identified needs. Every time you call an agency, record the date, name, and address of the agency, along with the name and telephone number of the contact person. Keep detailed notes on eligibility criteria, geographic area served, how to apply for services, and the cost.

Explore Eligibility Criteria, Fees, and Options   Find out who is eligible to receive specific services and how eligibility is verified. Discuss fees for services and exactly what the fees cover, exploring hidden costs.

Investigate options   Ask agency representatives if there are any other types of services that can meet the needs being discussed. For example, if the concern is for the safety of an older person who is alone during the day, the options might include friendly visitors, telephone reassurance, a personal emergency response system, or an adult day-care center. Ask for referrals to other organizations that provide similar services.

Get Written Confirmation   Ask the service representative to confirm your discussion in writing. Most agencies have written materials that describe their services.

Be Prepared For Intake Interviews   Some services require a face-to-face interview during which applications are completed, information is verified, and a needs assessment is conducted. Most community-based programs require that the older person, and sometimes the caregiver, apply in person at the location of the service. Most home-based services will conduct interviews over the telephone or in the home of the person who will be receiving the service.

Consumers should verify in advance what documentation is needed to complete the application process. If the agency needs to make copies of important papers, be sure all documentation is returned after being duplicated.

Be Persistent   Begin by understanding that you may get transferred from person to person. The first person who answers the telephone is usually a receptionist who may or may not be skilled at directing public inquiries. Before being transferred, ask for the name and telephone number of the person to whom you need to speak. Although you may be transferred several times, and perhaps even be disconnected, persistence equals success.

Monitor Formal Services   After a service has been put into place, caregivers need to monitor the service being provided. If not satisfied with a particular service, speak directly with the provider. If the problem persists, talk with the worker's supervisor. The next step is to write a letter to the agency's director.

On the other hand, if a service is satisfactory, be sure to let the worker and the supervisor know. Service workers welcome positive feedback, which helps create a bond that may result in a good working relationship.

References

American Association of Retired Persons (AARP). *Care Management: Arranging for Long-Term Care*. Washington, DC: AARP, 1989.

AARP. *Miles Away and Still Caring: A Guide for Long-Distance Caregivers*. Washington, DC: AARP, 1986.

AARP, and the Travelers Companies Foundation. *A National Survey of Caregivers*. Washington, DC: AARP, 1988.

AARP Public Policy Institute. *Medicare's Home Health Benefits: Eligibility, Utilization, and Expenditures Issue Brief*. Washington, DC: AARP, 1991.

Gillespie, Ann E., and Katrinka Sloan. *Housing Options and Services for Older Adults. Choices and Challenges*. Santa Barbara, CA: ABC-CLIO, 1990.

Lidoff, Lorraine. *Caregiver Support Groups in America*. Washington, DC: National Council on Aging, 1990.

Dow, Marion Merrill. *Managed Care Digest: Long-Term Care Edition*. Kansas City, MO: Marion Merrell Dow, 1991.

Springer, Dianne, and Timothy H. Brubaker. *Family Caregivers and Dependent Elderly: Minimizing Stress and Maximizing Independence*. Beverly Hills, CA: Sage Publications, in cooperation with the University of Michigan School of Social Work, 1984.

U.S. Department of Health and Human Services, Agency for Health Care Policy and Research. *Use of Home and Community Services by Persons Age 65 and Older with Functional Difficulties* Research Finding 5, DHHS publication no. 90-3466. Washington, DC: U.S. Department of Health and Human Services, September 1990.

Chapter 4

Planning for Financial, Legal, and Insurance Issues

Introduction

Many caregivers find it very difficult to discuss financial, legal, or insurance issues with the older persons they are caring for, let alone talk about these issues with anyone. For many people in both generations, topics relating to planning for the possibility of an older person's physical or mental decline or death are taboo. The older person may feel that these personal matters are nobody else's business, especially someone younger, such as an adult child, an adult relative, or an adult friend. In some cases, the older person would not even broach these subjects with a friend. The older person may also feel that he/she is able to handle these matters and that there is plenty of time with no need to rush into planning, often caused by an underlying fear that doing any definite planning may bring about his/her mental or physical decline.

But caregivers may become responsible for managing the older person's personal and business affairs and for making decisions about medical treatment and other end-of-life issues. It is urgent that they know about the care receiver's legal, insurance, and financial affairs. While caregivers want to be prepared for the future, they do not want to be viewed as prying, trying to take over, or implying that the older person is incompetent. For both the caregiver and the elderly person, the idea of getting older has emotional implications, including fear of dependency, loss of control, and a shift of roles in decision making.

Financial, legal, and insurance issues discussed in this chapter include what will be done in the case of the older person's mental or physical incapacity, long-term illness, terminal illness, and need for caregiving. Issues relating to illness and medical treatment include medical and long-term care insurance and legal documents such as living wills, durable power of attorney for health care, and other documents that allow the person's wishes to be respected and followed. Legal issues include the organization of necessary documents, records, and planning tools. Issues related to death include estate planning, wills, funeral arrangements, and wishes about life support.

Planning ahead and taking the necessary steps to put plans in place before any important decision has to be made will make these decisions easier and more satisfactory for both sides. Accepting the issues that need to be discussed, and deciding on arrangements while they are still fully able, allows older people to maintain control over their lives. It also gives the caregiver the information necessary to fulfill the older person's wishes, which should be the primary goal of planning.

Planning gives both parties a complete picture of what protective measures are in place and what issues the older person feels are important. Preplanning lets caregivers know what is expected of them. If all potential situations have been reviewed, and appropriate measures and procedures agreed on and taken, then when a difficult time or a crisis occurs, the agreed-on decisions and procedures are in place. Good planning gives caregivers and the elderly guidelines, directions, and roadmaps through the maze of financial, legal, and medical issues that they may encounter.

FACTS

- Only about three out of every ten Americans actually prepare a written will, even though most people recognize the importance of having one. A large majority of people therefore die intestate, or without a will.

- A trust is the most versatile tool for arranging assets, and it can be tailored to fit specific needs. Trusts are flexible, adaptable planning tools useful to people of any financial means.

- Most states have some form of Living Will, right-to-die, or natural death legislation.

- The U.S. Department of Health and Human Services estimates that more than 6 million people under age 65 are financially devastated by a catastrophic health incident every year.

- Almost 1 million families have at least one member who was refused medical treatment last year because of inadequate funds or lack of medical insurance.

Case Studies

Mollie Brown, after being widowed at 71, lived in her own apartment, had an active social life, did volunteer work, and took care of all her own financial affairs. Her two daughters felt fortunate that their mother was still independent and capable. She took trips and was a good role model for her daughters.

Then at age 77, during a long operation under general anesthesia, Mollie suffered a lack of oxygen to her brain. She lost her long-term memory immediately. In her spunky, no-nonsense manner, she took notes and rebuilt some of her memory, such as memory of her family relationships. After convalescing at her older daughter's home, she decided to go back to her apartment 40 miles away and to live independently. For a few years she managed, with unobtrusive support from her older daughter, a part-time aide, and adjustments in her apartment and way of living. When her short-term memory began to slip, she and her family worried together about her changing condition.

Mollie signed a living will she had copied years earlier from a magazine and gave copies to her daughters. The family discussed Mollie's wishes about the living will, which was not legally binding in her state at that time, and then discussed preparing a durable power of attorney, prepaying for a funeral, revising Mollie's medical insurance, and consolidating her savings accounts and other assets. Mollie said she wanted all of her affairs organized and in order, just the way her husband had taken care of everything before his death. When her medical insurance was reviewed the family discovered that she had adequate Medigap insurance but was not eligible for the few long-term care insurance policies then available.

The older daughter, as the primary caregiver, had a Durable Power of Attorney drawn up and she and her mother signed it. That document, plus other necessary legal papers, was placed in the caregiver's safe deposit box. Mollie's bank accounts were consolidated into a joint account with her older daughter, and the funeral was prearranged according to Mollie's wishes. When she died 18 years later, the family members felt they had given Mollie the care she needed in a way that she approved of and had protected her decision-making ability even after her mind further deteriorated.

At age 70, Laura Jackson had a stroke that left her without speech and with partial paralysis on her right side. While she was in the rehabilitation hospital, her family realized they should have legal access to Laura's bank accounts in case the funds were needed for her care or her funeral. But none of the family members was comfortable talking about such things with Laura because they feared she would feel they were giving up on her.

Laura moved in with Pat, her oldest daughter, and regained some use of her right side but not her speech. Several years later she showed signs of dementia, perhaps the early stages of Alzheimer's disease, and the family again began talking of what they should do about her bank account and her house, which was being rented. Before any action was decided upon, Laura had another stroke, which left her completely bedridden, incontinent, and in need of 24-hour care. After her hospitalization the family agreed to move her to a nursing home.

With no access to legal documents, the family had to seek court intervention to use Laura's assets to pay for her care. They had to pay Laura's medical bills, obtain a bank loan, and go through a traumatic court procedure for guardianship.

Harry Davis, a retired accountant with savings and a pension, refused to ask anyone for advice or help. A widower with no children, he had an extended family, friends, and a close relationship with his lawyer. But, being stubborn, a worrier, and a delayer, he made no plans for his later years because he did not like discussing "such unpleasant matters." His attitude was that the laws were bound to be changed and he had plenty of time.

On the few times he started a discussion with his lawyer about his future, Harry worried over so many details that nothing substantive was ever put on paper. Later, when he needed someone to act as a caregiver and make financial and medical decisions, there was no documentation and the court appointed a guardian to act on Harry's behalf.

Important Documents and Planning Tools

Planning ahead and getting organized for the care receiver's future is not only a prudent course of action, but a form of insurance, like automobile or fire insurance. You may hope you will never have to use it, but there is security in having it.

After an initial review of the issues, it is time to start a discussion with the older person. If a discussion could become unpleasant or unproductive, a third party who is aware of the issues and whom both the older person and the caregiver respect can act as a mediator. This person can also help keep the discussion on the issues and away from areas that might create ill feelings.

The Checklist of Important Documents and Information in Figure 2 provides a place to list the names, addresses, and telephone numbers that should be easily available to caregivers and family members. This list can be reviewed item by item and notes made as to whether the older person has the document and, if so, where it is kept. If the older person has not taken any steps toward acquiring these documents, now is the time to discuss doing so.

If the older person does not have a lawyer, he or she should seek an attorney clinic, or legal service that specializes in elder law. Elder law is a distinctive specialty; clients' needs go beyond the conventional tools of the legal system to include services such as counseling, legal drafting, negotiation, and litigation. The older client needs a comprehensive plan that provides for present and future physical, medical, and financial needs. The attorney may also be involved with the family or friends of the older person. Elder law specialists have knowledge of Social Security, SSI, veterans' benefits, Medicare, Medicaid, and the whole spectrum of health-care issues, including federal and state regulations of nursing homes, home care, and other alternatives to institutionalization.

An attorney should be knowledgeable about legal documents such as Advance Medical Directives, state laws on the Living Will, Durable Power of Attorney, and the state's guardianship laws. Elder law also covers financial, estate, and tax planning for the elderly. The plan should be prepared with consideration of what kinds of insurance are available, which investments are

General Medical Information

Names, addresses, and telephone numbers of
     All attending physicians
     Primary care doctor
     Specialists

1. _____

2. _____

3. _____

     Pharmacist _____
     Dentist _____
     Ambulance telephone number _____
     Hospital telephone number _____
     Hospital emergency room telephone number _____
     Medicare identification number _____
     Medicaid identification number (if applicable) _____

Names, addresses, and telephone numbers of any public or private agency currently giving some type of home care

1. _____

2. _____

3. _____

Personal Information

List locations of
     Birth certificate
     Names of parents
     Citizenship papers
     Education records
     Employment history
     Marriage license
     Divorce decree
     Separation agreement
     Social Security card
     Supplemental Security Income (SSI)
     Military service records
     Passports
     Memberships in organizations

Names, addresses, and telephone numbers of friends to contact in case of an emergency

Figure 2   Checklist of Important Documents and Information

Figure 2   (continued)

1. _____

2. _____

3. _____

4. _____

Financial Information and Records

Names, addresses, and telephone numbers of institutions and contact person or department in charge of the following and, when applicable, names listed on the documents

Checking accounts _____
Savings accounts of all types _____
IRAs/Keogh _____
Safe deposit box (bank and box number) and location of key _____
Trusts _____
Credit cards (numbers) _____
Automobile registration _____
Home, auto, boat mortgages (location of these documents) _____
Sources of income and assets _____
Liabilities (including mortgages, taxes, etc.) _____
Copies of recent income tax returns _____
Location of personal items (jewelry, family heirlooms) _____

Legal Documents

Include location and date made

Will _____
Living Will _____
Durable Power of Attorney _____
Funeral arrangements _____
Organ donation agreement _____
Advance Medical Directives _____
Insurance policies _____
    1. Life _____
    2. Medigap _____
    3. Long-term care _____
    4. Other _____

Employment-Related Documents

Names, addresses, telephone numbers, and contact person or department of previous and present employers (if applicable) to assist with

Life insurance _____
Medical insurance _____
Veteran benefits (if applicable) _____
Pension benefits _____

Figure 2   (continued)

IRA account with employer _____
Profit-sharing plan _____
Stock option plans _____
Credit union _____

Other Applicable Documents

1. _____

2. _____

3. _____

4._____

Professionals

Names, addresses, and telephone numbers of

Lawyer
Accountant
Insurance agent
Financial planner
Others

1. _____

2. _____

3. _____

suitable for the elderly client, and awareness of legal constraints on trust drafting, administration, and taxation.

Attorneys specializing in elder law handle emotionally difficult matters relating to love and loss, life and death, and the diminishing of clients' social status and physical capabilities. In this complex setting, the attorney is often involved, not only with the client, but with an accountant, hospital discharge planner, gerontologist, primary care physician, social worker, the caregiver, the family, and friends. All older people and their caregivers who want to ensure control of decisions that will affect both the quality of life and the wishes of the older person, not just those with large estates, can make use of an elder law attorney.

Many communities have legal aid services with staff lawyers who specialize in elder law. The local Area Agency on Aging

(AAA) or the state department on aging can direct people to these services. The telephone book lists the AAA under Human Services or Social Services. The social work department of a hospital is another source for information about lawyers. Chapter 8 lists other resources.

Legal clinics also offer help with simple legal matters such as writing a will. Legal clinics usually charge much lower fees than those of a standard law practice. To help keep the costs down for their clients, legal clinics employ a staff of paralegals. Volunteer lawyer projects also provide legal assistance to low-income elderly people. Lawyers volunteer their time and expertise on a variety of legal issues from drawing up wills to help with SSI and Medicaid requirements. Many of these volunteer lawyer projects are assisted by the AARP's Legal Counsel for the Elderly (LCE).

Another service in some communities is a Senior Judicare Program (or Project) where legal services are offered on a sliding scale basis and eligibility is based on the client's income. Since these are usually part of a city's services for the elderly, information about them can be obtained from the local AAA.

To find a private attorney who specializes in elder law, try the local bar association for a referral, or write to the American Bar Association Commission on Legal Problems of the Elderly. Addresses and information on these sources can be found in Chapter 8.

Some older people wish to use a professional financial planner, planning department of a bank, or an accountant to help organize and plan financial goals and priorities. Professional financial planning services charge an initial fee, depending on the income and net worth of the client, the planner's experience and expertise, and whether the planner charges a commission. Since many people call themselves financial planners, it is best to choose one who is certified. The initials CFP (Certified Financial Planner) following a name mean that the person is certified by the College of Financial Planning in Denver. The American College in Bryn Mawr, Pennsylvania, gives certification for chartered financial consultants (ChFC). A chartered life underwriter (CLU) is knowledgeable about insurance needs, and a certified public accountant (CPA) can give advice as an accountant and as a tax consultant.

Copies of the important documents and planning tools listed in Figure 2 should be kept in an accessible place, with the originals in a safe deposit box or with a lawyer. All legal documents should be reviewed periodically. Check your state laws and consult with a lawyer or a legal service if you need help preparing these documents. Also, check with your lawyer or a legal service for your state's laws on how often legal documents are to be reviewed. Since family and life situations change, it is prudent to reevaluate one's documents.

Letter of Instruction

A Letter of Instruction is a listing of essential information that includes a list of key documents and their location. The Letter of Instruction's purpose is to give another person information to be able to conduct the letter writer's affairs if necessary. While not a legal document, it should be in agreement with the terms of the person's will. The Letter of Instruction can be changed as often as the person wishes. Copies of it can be given to anyone the letter writer chooses, such as family members, friends, a lawyer, or an accountant.

Durable Power of Attorney

This legal document gives a person named as the older person's agent the power to act on his or her behalf. It differs from a general power of attorney in that it is not revoked if the person who made the power of attorney (the principal) becomes incompetent. State laws permit a power of attorney to be durable, which means that the power created by the document will not be affected by the principal's becoming incompetent. This must be stated in the document so that surrogate decisions can be made during an incapacity. In some states a springing power of attorney is created, which means it springs into action only when the principal becomes incompetent.

A Durable Power of Attorney can be written in any way the principal wishes. It can permit very limited or very broad responsibilities and cover large areas of decision making for financial affairs. The principal does not give up decision-making power by having a Durable Power of Attorney. The document appoints an agent or deputy to act only under certain specified conditions. A Durable Power of Attorney may be revoked by the principal as long as that person is competent to act. On the death of the principal, the power is automatically revoked.

Will

Why does one need a will? To quote the financial columnist Jane Bryant Quinn, "You own stuff, you will die. Someone will get your stuff." Anyone who has preferences about who gets what needs a will. A will is a legal document expressing an individual's wishes regarding the distribution or sale of his or her property. It controls the property that a person owns at the time of death. The original will should be stored in a safe deposit box or a lawyer's office. If copies are made of the will, then every copy must be produced in court when the will is filed. If the copies are not produced with the original, the law assumes the will was revoked.

There are many advantages to writing a will: It makes a person's wishes known, and it can save money in taxes as well as time in aggravation and administration. The disadvantage is the cost to have a will written by a lawyer or legal clinic.

Wills should be reviewed every three or five years, or when there is a major change in the author's life such as a divorce, death of a beneficiary, or a move to another state. Wills written before 1981 should be reviewed by a lawyer who specializes in estate planning since they may be affected by the Economic Recovery Act of 1981, which caused substantial changes in the laws regarding estate taxes. Other factors that make it advisable to review a will are a change of mind, changes in assets, an inheritance that was not covered in the present will, or new laws that mandate changes.

Some people believe a will is not necessary if they have a small estate. They may argue that they don't want to incur the cost of writing a will, that they will prepare one later, or that it is depressing to think about a will. Nonetheless, everyone should have a will. If a person dies without a will, called dying "intestate," the estate then passes under the estate's rules of "intestacy." Each state has specific rules about what happens to those estates of people who die without wills. In essence then, the state makes the will, which can lead to the disbursement of the estate and to situations that the deceased person would not have wanted. Dispersement and future use of the estate, regardless of its size, are placed under the control of the state.

Appointment of a Guardian or Conservator

Guardians or conservators are people appointed by the courts to assume responsibility for another person, called the ward, whom the courts have found to be incapacitated or incompetent to make rational decisions and understand their consequences. When no one has been given the legal authority to act on behalf of the incapacitated or incompetent person, the courts must be asked to appoint someone to assume the responsibility for health care and or financial matters.

While the legal terms vary from state to state, there are generally two forms of guardianship. In one form, the responsible person is called a guardian and in the other form a conservator. Usually, a guardian is someone with the legal authority to make personal and health care decisions regarding the ward's physical person. Guardians have the same rights, powers, duties, and responsibilities toward wards that parents have for their minor children, except that they are not required to use their own money to support the wards. A conservator is generally someone appointed by the courts to handle the financial affairs of the ward. The conservator takes possession of all the ward's assets and must protect, invest, and use them for the protected person's benefit. A person may need a guardian or a conservator or both, and the same person can be appointed to fill both positions.

Guardians and conservators have great power. A guardian can determine where the ward will live, what medical treatment the ward will or will not receive, whom the ward can associate with, whether the ward can marry or vote, and other aspects of the ward's life. In essence, the ward loses the right of self-determination. In taking control of all the assets, conservators receive all income. They decide if the protected person can have any spending money. The ward cannot sell assets or decide how they should be invested without the consent of the conservator.

Courts do not appoint guardians and conservators in a casual manner. Before any action, the person must be given notice of a petition that asks the court to act. The person then has the right to be present at the petition, the right to present and cross-examine witnesses, and, in most states, the right to a court-appointed attorney if financially unable to hire one. After a guardian and or conservator have been appointed they must present an accounting and reports for review. The court periodically reviews the need for the continuation of the guardianship or conservatorship. Laws and regulations for guardianship and conservatorship vary from state to state. Some states provide for a limited, temporary, or emergency guardianship. In some states a person does not have to be declared incompetent to have a conservator appointed, and in others a conservatorship can be requested by the person who needs help as well as by others interested in his or her needs. A person appointed in this capacity may also be known as a guardian of the person, guardian of the estate, conservator of the person, conservator of the estate, or curator and committee.

Declaring someone incompetent is a very dramatic and restrictive form of legal intervention to impose on an elderly person. With planning and foresight, elderly people can arrange for forms of surrogate decision making that they prefer, and have their wishes declared in a legal, written form to be used in the event that they become incapacitated or incompetent.

Trusts

A trust is a legal arrangement in which the ownership of assets is transferred by one person (the grantor, settlor, or trustor) to benefit himself or herself or someone else (the beneficiary). The trust is managed by a third person (the trustee) and is limited by whatever restrictions the grantor includes in the trust agreement. There are two types of trusts: testamentary and living.

The testamentary trust is a provision of a will and does not take effect and start paying dividends until the grantor dies. The testementary trust does not avoid probate, which is the procedure required by law for the judicial determination of the validity of a will by the court having jurisdiction to accept or reject the instrument as being the will of the decedent. What a testementary trust does do is to assure the grantor that an inheritance will be managed according to his or her wishes.

The living trust (also called *inter vivos*) is an agreement between living persons and can go into effect during the grantor's lifetime. Living trusts can be revocable or irrevocable. In a revocable living trust, the grantor has the power to dissolve or change the trust. An irrevocable living trust is permanent and unchangeable once the trust has begun. These trusts have special tax treatments.

Aside from living and testamentary trusts there are other types of trusts for different purposes, such as sprinkling, accumulated, standby, irrevocable life insurance trusts, Medicaid, and supplemental benefits or luxury trusts. All of these trusts are governed by state laws, and they should be written to conform to those laws and to meet the specific needs and preferences of the person setting up the trust. Attorneys, accountants, financial planners, and other advisors can help the older person review the options, laws, and what is best for the individual situation. As with any legal document, a trust needs to be reviewed regularly as laws and family or financial circumstances change.

Advance Medical Directives

By the late 1960s, the development of life-extending medical technologies made it possible for people to survive illnesses and injuries that formerly were fatal. Some people believe that this technology often gives patients a greater quantity of life, but not necessarily a greater quality of life. This technology meant that dying a natural death could no longer be taken for granted.

Life-support technology also raised the question of who could decide to end these so-called heroic measures once they were begun. The informal arrangement between the patient's family and the physician to make these difficult decisions no longer exists because of questions of legal liability and a changing relationship between the patient and the physician. For these reasons, new legal tools were developed to give someone authority to make and enforce an individual's preference in the event of his or her inability to make a decision about life support.

The most familiar document is the Living Will, but documents known as Advance Medical Directives also ensure that a person has made his or her medical directives or wishes known legally. These documents are of no value if no one knows they exist.

Therefore, a person who has signed a Living Will or Advance Medical Directive should tell or give copies to physicians, family members, friends, and others who may be involved in life-support decisions.

Living Will

A Living Will is a document signed by a person in a competent state that delineates his or her wishes regarding life-sustaining procedures should the person no longer be able to express them. A Living Will specifies what care one wishes given and not given if in a terminal situation or, in some states, if in a permanent vegetative state with no hope of regaining consciousness. The Living Will can be a simple declaration of a few sentences or be a more detailed statement of choices made under a variety of medical options and situations. No set language has been accepted by all the states. However, even in a state that has no Living Will legislation, executing even a simple Living Will document generally has force under the law.

Since states vary on the wording they require for a Living Will, it makes sense to draw up both a general and a specific state-approved form. If someone should have an accident away from the home state and be left permanently unconscious, a Living Will executed according to his or her state's language restrictions may not apply, while a more generally phrased one may. It is best to follow the home state's language requirements and the suggested renewal terms. States are moving quickly to pass legislation on Living Wills. Those who favor a Living Will need to keep up on their state's laws and any changes that occur.

Health Care Proxy

Two other documents are important to older people and their caregivers. Both these documents allow someone to be appointed to speak on medical matters for a person who is no longer able to communicate his or her own wishes. One is a Health Care Proxy and the other is a Durable Power of Attorney for Health Care.

A Health Care Proxy is normally designated in a state's Living Will legislation and is part of the Living Will form itself. The proxy can be limited by the state's Living Will statutes.

Durable Power of Attorney for Health Care

This legal document appoints a guardian (or agent) to make decisions on a patient's behalf should that patient become incompetent or unable to speak for himself or herself. The guardian or agent named in the document is expected to be familiar with the patient's wishes and to make decisions that the patient would want and approve.

A Durable Power of Attorney for Health Care usually has more authority than a proxy and, in some cases, more than a Living Will. Under a durable power, the agent is always able to represent the principal (the patient), even if the principal becomes incompetent. The Durable Power of Attorney applies to all medical decisions, unless the principal has specified limitations. Specific instructions for treatment to be given or refused, or whatever issues the principal wishes to include can be written into the document. Successor agents can be named should the primary agent be unable to act. This flexibility gives the Durable Power of Attorney for Health Care more control over the patient's medical treatment than that of a Health Care proxy or the Living Will.

Personal Medical Mandate

This document is a variation of the Living Will that goes into more specific details as to what types of treatment the patient does or does not want. This document was proposed as a new type of Advance Medical Directive by two physicians writing in the *Journal of the American Medical Association*. The purpose of a Personal Medical Mandate is to provide doctors with specifics so that they can better understand the wishes of their patients.

The Personal Medical Mandate is designed to protect patients who become unable to communicate their wishes. This type of document would be difficult to implement on a national basis since legislative language regarding Advance Medical Directives is not standardized. Patients or their caregivers could ask their doctors and hospitals if they have developed a Personal Medical Mandate. If there is one, its use can encourage a good patient-physician discussion. Samples of the various types of documents regarding medical and health care decisions can be found in some of the References listed at the end of this chapter.

Personal Records

Vital information should be gathered and made accessible before a crisis arises. While each situation is different and may require information that is not covered on the Checklist of Important Documents and Information in Figure 2, the suggestions there give an idea of what type of information may be needed.

Financial Records

Going over the checklist in Figure 2 will help older people and caregivers organize information and locate documents that may be scattered around, misplaced, or lost. Some of these documents may need to be reviewed, updated, or changed.

Insurance: Medicare, Medicaid, and Medigap

These three words are often misunderstood by older people and their families and friends. Medicare and Medicaid are two major health care programs provided by the federal government. The Medicare program is for the elderly and disabled, and Medicaid offers financial assistance for medical care to certain low-income people.

Medicare is the health insurance component of Social Security administered by the federal government for people 65 or older and for some disabled people under 65. Most people apply for Medicare automatically when they apply for Social Security benefits at age 65. If they retire before or after 65, they can apply for Medicare separately. Almost everyone can enroll for Part B of Medicare at age 65 and pay the monthly premiums.

Medicare

The Medicare program is a federal health insurance program primarily designed for individuals entitled to Social Security who are age 65 or older and for some disabled persons under the age of 65. Medicare is divided into two parts: Part A is hospital insurance, and Part B is supplementary medical insurance. Certain services and items are not covered under either part, such as services considered custodial care and those that Medicare has determined not to be reasonable and necessary. Since Medicare changes its guidelines and requirements every year, recipients should keep up with changes and, if in doubt, get help from the organization that handles their Medicare claim, the social service department of a local hospital, or the Area Agency on Aging.

Part A of Medicare covers most inpatient hospital services and limited nursing home, hospice, and home-health care. Part B covers doctors' services provided in or out of a hospital, emergency room or clinic services not provided during a hospital stay (also called outpatient care), and some other services and supplies not covered under Part A, such as some medical equipment, ambulance trips, and emergencies. Patients must pay deductibles, copayments, and any expenses not covered by Medicare. Part A is financed through part of the social security (FICA) tax paid by all workers and their employers. Part A benefits are provided automatically on the basis of prior work. The monthly premium for Part A does not have to be paid if the person or the spouse are entitled to benefits under either the Social Security or the Railroad Retirement systems, or if the person or their spouse has worked for a sufficient period of time in federal, state, or local government to be insured. If the person, at age 65, does not have enough work credits or does not meet the qualifications for premium-free Part A benefits, that person may purchase Part A coverage, if they are at least age 65, by signing up at the local Social Security office during the three months immediately before reaching age 65 or during the first three months of any year thereafter. The Part A premium for 1992 is $192 per month. Part B benefits are available only if the person pays the monthly premiums. About 95 percent of those who are eligible elect to pay for Part B benefits.

The Medicare program helps pay only for covered services that are determined by Medicare to be medically necessary. And it must be understood that Medicare usually does not pay the full cost of the covered services.

Medicaid

Medicaid is a federal- and state-funded social welfare program that pays for certain medical care costs of poor, disabled, or aged people. Needy older people can have their Medicare deductibles and copayments paid by Medicaid.

Medicaid programs are administered by each state's government. Requirements vary from state to state, as each state has its own eligibility and coverage rules, creating 51 different Medicaid programs. For example, people eligible for Medicaid assistance for nursing home expenses in one state may not be eligible for the same assistance in another state. In most states, eligible individuals include elderly people who receive Supplemental Security Income (SSI) or the elderly in need of nursing home care whose income and resources meet the state's limits. The local AAA, welfare department, or the social service department of a hospital or nursing home can explain the various criteria for Medicaid assistance with nursing home care.

Medigap Insurance

Insurance companies offer supplemental policies to help pay the "gaps" not covered by Medicare. As of July 1992 all states are required by law to meet certain standards for Medigap insurance. This law, passed by Congress in 1990, protects consumers by restricting unfair sales practices and simplifies policies by limiting the types of plans that can be sold and specifying the benefits each plan must offer. All Medigap policies now must match one of ten standardized plans, labeled A through J. Insurance companies are not required to offer all ten plans approved for sale by each state, but they must make Plan A available in order to sell any of the other nine plans. To find out which Medigap policies are available, contact your State Department of Aging, State Insurance Commission, Medicare office or Area Agency on Aging. For those who cannot afford a Medigap policy, contact the Medicare office or 800-638-6833 for information about the Qualified Medicare Beneficiary (QMB) program.

Long-Term Care Insurance

Even Medigap policies may leave large gaps in coverage of health care services, and the most significant of these gaps is coverage of long-term care. This phrase usually refers to a long stay in a nursing home for intermediate or custodial care rather than for skilled nursing care. An example of such care is that given Alzheimer's disease patients and those with other forms of dementia. Stroke patients are another group that often require extensive care and rehabilitation in a nursing home.

Medicare only pays for about 2 percent of all nursing home care and about 4 percent of home-health care. Some 50 percent of nursing home care is paid for by patients and their families from out-of-pocket resources. Many patients run out of money and then become eligible for Medicaid. It is estimated that about 42 percent of all nursing home care costs are paid for by Medicaid.

To fill this gap, insurance companies offer policies to protect the consumer against such long-term care costs. These policies are designed to pay for the care needed by people with a chronic illness or a long-term disability. Many policies offer care either in the home or in an institutional setting.

The cost of the policy probably is the biggest factor in the decision whether to purchase a long-term care insurance policy. Long-term care policies are expensive and may be out of the reach of people on a fixed income. These policies are changing rapidly as the market for them grows, and the benefits they offer are improving. Consult Figure 3, Questions To Ask about Long-Term Care Insurance, or up-to-date articles and books on how to evaluate these policies and what to ask when reviewing them.

Since there are no federal regulations or standards for long-term care insurance, the National Association of Insurance Commissioners (NAIC) has developed some model regulations. About half of the states have adopted the NAIC model.

1. An outline of coverage as a part of the standard policy disclosure must be provided to policyholders. This document, separate from the policy, must be printed in a readable size of type and give a brief description of the important features of the policy. This outline is useful for comparing policies.

2. The person who buys a policy from an insurance agent must have the right to return it within 30 days of receipt and have the premium refunded, if the policyholder is not satisfied for any reason after examining the policy.

1. What kind of care (service) is covered?
    a. Skilled nursing care
    b. Intermediate care
    c. Custodial care
    d. Home-health care
    e. Adult day care

2. How much does the policy pay per day for each level of care?

3. How long will the policy pay benefits for each level of care?

4. Does the policy have a maximum lifetime benefit? If yes, what is it for nursing home care? For home-health care?

5. Are preexisting conditions covered? If yes, what is the waiting period? Is the waiting period different for various conditions?

6. Is there an inflation adjustment in the policy? Will benefits increase with inflation?

7. How many days must the policyholder wait before benefits can begin?

8. What is the maximum amount that will be paid for each claim? How is it calculated—for example, is it a dollar figure, or is it for the time period the policyholder is in a nursing home? The policy could be worded, "This policy will not pay any more benefits after two years in a nursing home."

9. How long will the policy's benefits last for the following?
    a. Skilled nursing care
    b. Intermediate nursing care
    c. Custodial nursing care
    d. Home-health care
    e. All of the above services

10. What is the maximum amount the policy will pay?

11. Does the policy impose any of the following eligibility requirements?
    a. Prior hospitalization to receive skilled nursing home care benefits
    b. Need for skilled nursing care prior to payment of custodial care costs
    c. Coverage only in a Medicare-certified facility
    d. Waiting period (also called an elimination or deductible)

12. Is Alzheimer's disease specifically covered? See also question 20, item f.

13. Can the insurer cancel the policy? Is the policy guaranteed renewable? Does the insurer have the sole option of cancellation? Guaranteed renewability means the policyholder has the right to continue the policy by payment of the premium and that the insurer cannot decline the renewal; this ensures lifetime coverage.

Figure 3   Questions To Ask about Long-Term Care Insurance

Figure 3   (continued)

14. If it is a group policy, who can terminate the policy? The individual? The group? The insurance company?

15. Will the premium increase over the life of the policy?

16. Does the policy contain a waiver of premium?

17. Is the insurer experienced in handling health insurance claims?

18. Does the insurer have an A+ or A rating from Best's Insurance Reports?

19. What is the annual premium?

20. What is specifically excluded from coverage?
    a. Expenses incurred outside of the United States
    b. Expenses due to a war or act of war
    c. Dental treatment unless due to accidental injuries
    d. Expenses from intentional, self-inflicted injuries
    e. Expenses caused by nonorganic psychological disorders such as depression and anxiety
    f. Expenses caused by organically based mental or nervous disorders such as Parkinson's disease, multiple sclerosis (MS), amyotrophic lateral sclerosis (ALS, commonly referred to as Lou Gehrig's disease), and forms of senility other than Alzheimer's.
    g. Care outside of your local area—i.e., services needed while on vacation, staying with friends or relatives in another area, or living in a vacation home

21. At what age can the policyholder obtain long-term care insurance?

22. Is there underwriting of the long-term care policy?

3. The person who has bought a long-term care insurance policy from a mail solicitation must have the right to return it within 30 days after its receipt and have the premium refunded, if the policyholder is not satisfied for any reason. This is known as the "free look."

4. These conditions should be eliminated:
   • Requirement of prior hospitalization
   • Conditionally renewable provisions
   • Exclusion of Alzheimer's disease and related disorders

The Health Insurance Association of America has a toll-free number for questions about health insurance policies including long-term care policies and an up-to-date informational booklet on long-term care policies (see Chapter 8). Other sources for information are the state insurance departments and state departments on aging.

Funeral Arrangements

Since the mortality rate of the human race is 100 percent, it is pointless to avoid discussing the subject of death and funerals. Given the emotional trauma of the many decisions that have to be made when someone close dies, it is important to be prepared to deal with this stressful event. Planning a funeral before death occurs will ease many of the difficult and emotional decisions for the survivors. It also allows the older person to arrange his or her funeral. Arrangements can be made involving professional funeral homes or nonprofit memorial societies.

Memorial Societies

These societies have existed in the United States since 1939. As nonprofit organizations they are staffed almost completely by volunteers. They advocate preplanning of funerals, freedom to conduct funerals to conform with one's religious beliefs and values, and an economical funeral.

Memorial societies do not sell or provide funeral services directly to their members. Instead they arrange contracts and agreements with funeral providers to take care of their members when a death occurs. In general, most memorial society members pay much less for funerals and cremations than do those who deal with the established funeral homes. The membership cost is low, with one-time dues. Many of these societies will transfer a membership if a member moves to another area. Most memorial societies belong to the Continental Association of Funeral and Memorial Societies, a nonprofit, nonsectarian, non-discriminatory organization that assures that its providers adhere to high standards. Information about memorial societies can be obtained by writing this association at 6900 Lost Lake Road, Egg Harbor, WI, 54209, or call (800) 458-5563 for general information or (414) 868-3136 for specific information.

Prepaid Funerals

Sometimes referred to as pre-need plans, these arrangements lock in the cost of the funeral, provide peace of mind, and ensure that survivors will not be burdened with either planning or costs of a funeral at the time of death. As with any other service, the prepayment plan has to be carefully examined. You must be sure that the provider will be in business when you need the funeral, and be sure to ask the following questions:

• If the consumer moves to another community, can the plan be transferred? If not, will there be a refund?

• Into what type of account is the pre-need fund placed?

• Will interest be drawn on the account?

• Does the contract specify that the type of funeral selected will be honored for the amount of money placed in the fund regardless of the costs at the time of death?

• Is there a time limit for making changes to the original agreement?

When a pre-need plan is bought, it is important to let the immediate family, friends, or caregiver know where the contract is and the name of the funeral home. The other method of preplanning is to prearrange all the details and set aside a bank account that draws interest to cover the estimated cost of the funeral.

Other Considerations after the Funeral

If the deceased person was collecting Social Security, survivors should call the local Social Security office to give notice of the death. The family can apply for the Social Security lump-sum death benefit and other survivor benefits that may be applicable, usually to the surviving spouse. Any benefit checks that were not cashed by the deceased should be returned.

If the person was a veteran, contact the regional office of the Veterans Administration to apply for survivor and burial benefits that may be available. If the person was an active or retired military member, contact the casualty assistance officer at the closest military installation for assistance in collecting survivor benefits and entitlements. Death benefit entitlements may also be received from civil service, trade unions, fraternal, and other organizations that the deceased belong to, if survivors pursue these sources.

References

American Association of Retired Persons (AARP). *Before You Buy—A Guide to Long-Term Care Insurance*. Washington, DC: AARP, 1991.

AARP. *Tomorrow's Choices: Preparing Now for Future Legal, Financial, and Health Care Decisions*. Washington, DC: AARP, 1988.

Emanuel, Linda, and Ezekiel Emanuel. "The Medical Directive: A New Comprehensive Advance Care Document." *Journal of the American Medical Association* 26, no. 22 (June 9, 1989): 3288–3293.

Myers, Teresa Schwab. *How To Keep Control of Your Life after 50: A Guide for Your Legal, Medical, and Financial Well-Being*. New York: Free Press, 1990.

Outerbridge, David E., and Alan R. Hersh. *Easing the Passage: A Guide for Pre-arranging and Ensuring a Pain-Free and Tranquil Death via a Living Will, Personal Medical Mandate, and Other Medical, Legal, and Ethical Resources*. New York: Harper Collins, 1991.

Sabatino, Charles P. *Health Care Power of Attorney: An Introduction and Sample Form*. Washington, DC: American Bar Association, 1990.

Skala, Ken. *American Guidance for Seniors*. 3rd ed. Falls Church, VA: American Guidance Inc., 1991.

Smith, Bradley E., and Jess Brallier. *Write Your Own Living Will*. New York: Crown, 1991.

Soled, Alex J. *The Essential Guide to Wills, Estates, Trusts and Death Taxes. An AARP Book*. Glenview, IL: Scott, Foresman, 1988.

Strauss, Peter J., et al. *Aging and the Law*. Chicago: Commerce Clearinghouse, 1990.

United Seniors Health Cooperative. *1992 Medicare and Medigap Update*. Washington, DC: USHC, 1992.

U.S. Department of Health and Human Services, Health Care Financing Administration. *1992 Guide to Health Insurance for People with Medicare*. Publication no. HCFA-02110 Washington, DC: GPO, 1992.

Chapter 5

Safety and Welfare

Introduction

As people age, they do not lose the desire to live in their own homes surrounded by belongings full of memories. Familiarity brings a sense of security and safety, a refuge where people can maintain their independence, privacy, and social relationships. For the elderly, staying in their own homes gives a sense of control, continued social status, and self-worth.

Caregiving is easier when the elderly person has a safe, familiar, and accessible living arrangement. Sometimes it may be necessary for the elderly person to move into a ground floor apartment, an assisted living community, or another living arrangement, as discussed in Chapter 6. But for many older people, staying in their own homes is possible, with some planning, alterations, and adjustments.

Houses were not designed to grow old with their human occupants, to accommodate human frailties, or to change on their own. Elderly occupants and their caregivers must plan alterations so that the house remains safe and comfortable. With common sense, they can change a home or apartment in order to age-proof the dwelling for physical safety and peace of mind.

As a team, the older person and the caregiver should review the living quarters. They can take a walking tour through all of the rooms and try to imagine how the resident's or residents' needs and activities may change in the future. Using the checklists in this chapter, they can plan to customize and age-proof the house or apartment. The caregiver should try, for a few hours, to see the living environment through the eyes and capabilities of the older person. With creativity and common sense, most living spaces can be altered to compensate for the occupants' changes in mobility, vision, hearing, and chronic medical conditions, and the physical surroundings be made as convenient, accessible, and safe as possible.

Most older Americans live in houses that were bought many years ago and that, more than likely, have outdated and inefficient heating equipment. Houses that are more than 20 years old may have inadequate insulation, leaking windows, inadequate wiring, and other problems. A number of guides, associations, and catalogues are available to help update and repair homes, as are home remodeling or retrofitting firms and a growing body of knowledge on appliances, furnishings, equipment, and creating homes free of barriers to people with disabilities.

As bodies age, the changes can make the activities of daily living more difficult. These problems are the challenges. This chapter discusses how to analyze the challenges and how to find information, solutions, ideas, and resources to help make the home environment as safe and comfortable as possible.

FACTS

- An American Association of Retired Persons (AARP) national survey conducted in 1986 found that 78 percent of the elderly did not want to move from their present dwellings. In 1989 a similar study reported that 86 percent of the elderly wanted to stay where they were. This shows an increase of 8 percent over a three-year period.

- Approximately 75 percent of the elderly own their own homes, with 80 percent of these homes being mortgage-free.

- According to the National Safety Council, 23,000 people over the age of 65 die every year from accidental injuries and another 750,000 become disabled. Although older people account for 12 percent of the population, they make up 21 percent of those who have had falls.

- The rate of death in fires for the older population is about five times higher than that of the general population.

- Older people are more accident-prone than any other age group because of impaired vision, slower reaction times, and poor balance.

- The rooms that have the highest accident rates are the kitchen and bathroom.

- The National Safety Bureau of Standards' Center for Fire Research estimates that smoke detectors could prevent 55 percent of fire deaths by alerting the residents before an escape becomes impossible.

Case Study

Mr. Reuter's son and daughter, both professionals with families of their own and active life-styles, decided that their father, an 80-year-old widower, should move out of his home. The children felt that he would be better off in a life-care retirement community or a personal care home. They believed the house was too big for their father and too crowded with furniture. In their view, the stairs were dark, the rugs and kitchen linoleum were old, and everything in the house seemed to creak, slide, or move. They worried that Mr. Reuter was too old to manage the house and care for himself, that he could not keep the house clean, that he cooked dull and boring meals, and that he must be very lonely.

The children contacted two residential facilities and the admissions offices sent people to review the house and the father's way of living. In both cases, the admissions people found Mr. Reuter an alert, active man who had no interest in their facilities and was very content with his life as it was. He enjoyed cooking his own meals, did not mind eating the same foods every day, and was not suffering from malnutrition. Mr. Reuter had his routines, his activities, and his friends. While the house was not in an impeccable condition, it was livable and reasonably clean.

Mr. Reuter was agreeable to making safety modifications and suggested a few of his own. The admissions people pointed out areas in the house that needed modification for safety and suggested the purchase of a personal emergency response system (PERS) to help ease their concerns. With these adjustments and modifications, Mr. Reuter stayed in his own home and retained his independence.

The above scenario demonstrates a solution that made an older person's home as safe and secure as possible while respecting his right to live as he chooses, to maintain his independence, and not to have another's vision of what is right imposed on him. Mr. Reuter was competent and able to care for himself, was comfortable with his life-style, and wished to continue living in his own home. While his children were concerned and caring, they were seeing his way of living through their own eyes instead of through his. They had not envisioned how the house could be age-proofed and modified to accommodate their father's needs.

Caregivers can show concern and offer help to the elderly person without causing hurt feelings and alienation. Both parties should go through the house together, role-playing the way the elderly person lives and his or her routines, and see if the house suits the life-style of the elderly person. The Checklist for Evaluating a House or Apartment in Figure 4 can be used as a guide to determine whether the home, its location, and maintenance meet the elderly person's needs. If both parties feel comfortable with the initial evaluation, then the house or apartment should be reviewed for areas that need repair or renovation or can be hazardous.

The books on home renovation listed at the end of this chapter have detailed checklists to help families evaluate the house or

Is the neighborhood safe?

Is there good public transportation?

Is there convenient shopping?

Are there adequate and conveniently located medical services?

Do friends and family members live nearby?

Are recreational activities nearby?

Is the house near the person's church or synagogue?

Are there adequate social services in the area?

Is the house in relatively good condition?

Do the elderly people feel comfortable in the house?

Is the maintenance of the house within the elderly person's budget, now and projecting for increased costs over time?

Is the insurance coverage manageable?

Figure 4   Checklist for Evaluating a House or Apartment

apartment and then decide what needs to be done. When removing barriers from houses, the costs of maintenance and utilities should be considered. Available safety devices and services provide security, immediate attention, and peace of mind for the older people and the caregivers. The books also help in setting priorities and organizing tasks.

While no two people age in the same way and at the same rate, there are many common physical changes that all experience. Changes that affect the ability to live in a physical setting meant for a younger person include vision loss, hearing loss, and limitations in mobility from a variety of causes such as arthritis, declining strength, and sensory capacity. But modifications, changes, and adaptations can make the environment friendlier and more supportive for the elderly person who is experiencing some of these changes.

Age-Proofing the House

To assess the changes needed to promote the independence and well-being of the elderly person and to prevent home accidents, first watch the daily routines of the elderly person, note potential problem areas, and ask the resident what changes would make daily living easier. After reviewing some checklists found in books on home renovation, make up your own lists of needed materials for repairs you think family members can conveniently do themselves. As with all aspects of caregiving, it is important to be realistic about what you can and cannot do.

With your lists in hand, visit some large hardware or home-products stores to look for items, materials, and ideas for ways to light rooms, stairways, halls, and closets. The service departments of local telephone, electric, or gas companies can also give ideas and suggestions, as can professionals in the remodeling and retrofitting fields.

Lighting

Inadequate lighting and glare can contribute to danger for the older person. Lighting can be improved by leaving curtains and blinds open during the day unless the exposure causes too much glare. In this case plastic products, such as tinted window-covering films, can help reduce the glare from the windows. Many are made for do-it-yourself installation. Glare can be further reduced by using frosted bulbs, indirect lighting, and shades or globes on light fixtures. In the kitchen and other work areas, install under-the-cabinet and over-the-countertop lighting. Always make sure to use the right type and wattage of bulbs for each fixture.

SAFETY RECOMMENDATIONS

The American Optometric Association offers these recommendations:

1. Maintain soft overall lighting indoors and use auxiliary lamps for tasks that require more light such as reading, sewing, cooking, or taking medications.

2. Incandescent lights may be more comfortable than fluorescent lights.

3. Lights should be easy to use. Light switches are best located at a room's entrance and at convenient heights. Light switches that are illuminated at night are also convenient.

4. Exterior lighting and lights at doors, garages, and stairs should have adequate wattage. Photoelectric lights that turn on automatically at dusk offer safety and security.

5. To compensate for diminished eyesight, older people may require up to three times as high a light-intensity level as a much younger person.

6. Night-lights are a good safety feature in hallways going from bedrooms to bathrooms and stairs, especially at the top and bottom steps.

7. Lights used for personal grooming and tasks such as reading labels or taking medications should shine directly on what is to be looked at rather than into the person's eyes. A direct light source can create a glare problem for people wearing glasses.

Stairways

Stairways are second only to bathrooms as a location of accidents. As people age, stairs become more difficult to use. Risers that are higher than 6–7 inches are difficult for many older people to climb, and risers over 8 inches create high steps that can cause the climber to stub a toe. Lighting is an important factor in stair safety. Even if the person is familiar with the stairs, adequate lighting can help prevent falls. The user should be able to turn lights on and off at both ends of the stairway.

SAFETY RECOMMENDATIONS

1. Open risers such as those found on outdoor stairs are hazardous because toes can get caught, causing the person to trip. Open risers can create spatial distortion for people with poor vision.

2. The tread of each step should be wide enough for the foot to rest completely on it. Carpeting any stair reduces the usable tread width to 8 or 7 inches, while the usual requirement for a tread width is 9 inches, less than the length of an adult foot. The tread can be built out by adding a beveled nosing to increase the tread to at least 11 inches, so that the entire foot can fit onto the tread even with carpeting. For additional safety, use a tightly woven carpet with no loops or high nap and for padding a ¼ inch thick dense (commercial) padding.

3. Handrails on both sides of the stairs give support by allowing people to use either or both hands while going up and coming down. Handrails at 36-inch height are better for support in case of a fall than the usual 32-inch height. Handrails should extend beyond the top and bottom steps to give the user support while getting on and off the last step.

4. Handrails should be installed far enough from the wall to allow adequate grabbing space for knuckles and fingers.

Halls

For elderly persons who use wheelchairs or may do so in the future, hallways should be at least 4 feet wide to allow for easier maneuvering and turning around. For those who are ambulatory, wide hallways make other tasks such as moving furniture easier. The installation of handrails on both sides of the hall provides security against falls or feelings of dizziness or disorientation. The handrails should be placed at a convenient height for the older person and far enough away from the wall for the hands to fit comfortably with adequate grabbing space. Refer to the sections on lighting when evaluating the hallways.

Although enlarging halls is not practical in most cases, there are simple ways to increase a hall's width and accessibility. If the hallway has protruding moldings at the base of the walls, these could be removed, gaining a few inches on both sides. Narrow doors (usually 32 inches) can be removed and replaced with a larger door (36 inch). The larger door is easier for a person in a wheelchair. Doors could also be removed and the openings widened without a new door being put in, depending on the layout of the house and the rooms that open onto the hall.

Floors

Since falls are the most common cause of fatal injuries for older people, the floors and their coverings need careful observation. Throw rugs, loose area rugs, and runners are major culprits leading to tripping and slipping. Rugs should be made slip-resistant or secured to the floor. These rugs are also great collectors of house dust and other contributors to allergy reactions, so they need frequent cleaning. Carpets or rugs with a low, tight pile are less likely to catch a heel and cause an accident than those with a high pile.

Check the floor levels in the house or apartment for changes such as going from a vinyl floor to a thickly carpeted floor. Other floor level changes include sunken living rooms, unusual architectural details, and the meeting of a tiled bathroom and a carpeted hallway. A great change in floor levels can create a danger spot.

Bathroom and kitchens floors can be covered with a nonslip floor covering. Ceramic tiles with such a finish can also be used in entry halls, basements, and other areas where water can accumulate. For additional safety, use nonskid mats in such wet areas as near kitchen or bathroom sinks, bathtubs, or shower stalls.

SAFETY RECOMMENDATIONS

1. Choose ceramic tiles with a nonslip finish for bathroom or kitchen flooring. These can also be used in entry halls and basements.

2. Carpeting with a low, tight pile is less likely to catch a heel and cause an accident than a carpet with a high pile.

3. Nonskid mats in areas that are often wet, such as entrances and near kitchen or bathroom sinks, bathtubs, or shower stalls, protect against falls and tripping.

Fire Safety

Smoke detectors are recommended for each level of the house. They should be placed on the ceiling or on a wall 12 inches below the ceiling. A smoke detector should never be placed in a corner where air cannot circulate. Smoke detectors should be at least 3 feet from heat registers and air ducts. They need to be placed near furnaces or heating equipment, in the garage, and in the kitchen.

All smoke detectors must be checked on a regular basis. Since fires often start at night, it is wise to place smoke detectors or fire alarms in the hallways that go to bedrooms or just outside the bedroom doors. Consider installing a fire extinguisher that is triple rated with the Underwriters' Laboratories (UL) or Factory Mutual (FM) seal of approval. The fire extinguisher's purpose is not to put out the fire, but to slow down the spread of flames, giving the residents more time to escape.

Fires can be started in kitchens if there are combustible items such as curtains, paper towels, and wall hangings near the stove. The simplest solution is to place these items away from the stove. Rearranging a kitchen is a delicate matter requiring tact, diplomacy, and understanding. Workrooms and hobby areas also may contain fire hazards such as electrical outlets that can be over-loaded, frayed cords that need replacement, and outlets, cords, and wiring that should be checked by an electrician.

Space heaters should be checked for grounding, placement, and proximity to combustible materials. Kerosene, gas, and LP gas heaters, as well as wood-burning stoves, must have adequate ventilation; the residents should use the correct fuel as recommended by the manufacturer and understand the operating instructions. A wood-burning stove should be installed only by a qualified person in accordance with the local building codes. Check fire insurance coverage for wood-burning stoves.

An emergency exit plan should be worked out with the elderly person as an important part of the fire safety plan. The fire exit plan can be drawn up and several copies displayed, perhaps framed, and equipped with night-lighting to help the residents remember the plan. Or the exit route can be marked on the floors and walls with luminous tape.

Kitchens and Bathrooms

These are the most used rooms of a house or apartment and the ones with the most safety hazards. Areas of concern have been mentioned in the sections on lighting, floors, and fire safety.

SAFETY RECOMMENDATIONS

1. Cooktop stoves and wall-mounted ovens are better for a barrier-free kitchen than a floor-standing range.

2. Electric stoves and ovens are recommended by many experts because there are no products of combustion such as carbon monoxide and no gas leaks that might be undetected by elders with an impaired sense of smell.

3. Cooktops should have controls at the front or side for easy accessibility to people who need to sit while cooking.

4. For safety, countertops and floors should be of different colors. A clean color break between the two

surfaces helps visually impaired people to distinguish where the counter edge ends.

5. In bathrooms and kitchens, use the ground fault circuit interrupter-type (GFCI) electrical outlets to protect against an electric shock.

6. A combination bathtub and shower is safer to use than a bathtub. Look for units that feature ease of entry and built-in or fold-up seating that can be moved or folded away.

7. Grab bars at the toilet, tub, and shower prevent falls. Flexible shower heads and lever-type faucets make bathing easier.

8. Oversized light switches or a lighted bathroom switch help increase bathroom safety.

9. D-shaped drawer pulls and knobs are best for gripping.

10. Turn the water thermostat down to prevent accidental scalding, or install a device to control water temperature.

11. Single-lever faucets are best because they provide a visual indication of water temperature and a mixed flow of water from a single tap.

12. Light colors are generally more cheerful and reflect more light.

Furniture and Room Arrangement

Open room arrangements that provide a straight-line entry are the safest. Place furniture and arrange traffic patterns to avoid air ducts in the floor. Planning a clear traffic flow is especially important for people who use a cane or walker, as is avoiding the clutter of small tables, hassocks, magazine racks, TV tables, and other low furnishings.

Frequent rearrangements of furniture can be unsafe. While variety may be the spice of life, it also destroys familiarity and habits that aid elderly people who have poor vision and failing agility. It is best to find a comfortable furniture arrangement with a good traffic flow and stay with it.

SAFETY RECOMMENDATIONS

1. Hallways should have a clear path for walking.

2. Storage shelves and cabinets should be arranged to minimize reaching and low bending.

3. Chairs and couches should be tested for ease of getting in and out. Unsteady furniture should be repaired or replaced.

Telephones

The telephone is a link to the outside world. This multifaceted tool, available in a large variety of styles, belongs in every room of the elderly person's house or apartment. The telephone offers security and communication to both the elderly person and the caregiver. Special telephones are available for the hard of hearing, for those with arthritic fingers, and for those with a vision loss.

SAFETY RECOMMENDATIONS

1. Telephones can be adapted for those with hearing losses by an amplified handset, signal devices, TTYs (teletypewriters), or extension bells. Local telephone companies can offer help through their special needs departments.

2. A template with large numbers can be put on top of telephones with hard-to-see numbers.

3. If the older person has difficulty dialing a rotary telephone, consider a push button or memory telephone.

4. Telephones installed in the bedroom, kitchen, living area, garage, or basement offer a sense of security.

5. A cordless telephone is useful for an elderly person in a wheelchair or for one who does gardening or other outside activities.

6. Put lists of emergency telephone numbers near all telephones. Write in large, clear, dark letters and numbers, and slip the lists into see-through plastic covers.

Appliances

SAFETY RECOMMENDATIONS

1. Appliances with lighted indicators to show when they are on offer a built-in safety feature. Some appliances, such as irons, also have an automatic shut-off. Lights can be used to supplement sound on doorbells, alarm clocks, and smoke alarms for the hearing impaired.

2. Power tools and electrical appliances need three-prong adapters to connect a three-prong plug to a two-hole receptacle.

3. Guards should be kept in place on power tools to avoid risk of injury from sharp edges or moving parts.

4. Place rechargeable flashlights in bedrooms, kitchens, basements, and garages.

Automobile Driving

Outside of the home, the automobile represents a vital link with the rest of the world and is a symbol of freedom and independence. Unfortunately, vehicle accidents are also a leading cause of accidental deaths among older people. The AARP and the National Retired Teachers Association (NRTA) recommend that older drivers be aware of changes in their reaction time and vision. Safe driving can be maintained if allowances are made for these physiological changes. The Driver's Self-Assessment Questionnaire in Figure 5 can help an elderly person become aware of his or her changing capabilities.

1. I get regular eye check-ups, and the doctor says I have good night vision, peripheral vision, and depth perception.

2. My medications have been evaluated for possible interactions or side effects that might affect my driving skills.

3. I am aware that over-the-counter medications can affect my driving skills.

4. I get comprehensive medical examinations on a regular basis and am checked for conditions that may affect my driving skills such as loss of hearing, flexibility, and muscle strength, or fatigue, emotional responses, and reaction responses.

5. My family and friends have hardly ever made critical comments or expressed concern about my driving. Be honest.

6. I have had fewer than two accidents in the past two years.

7. I have received no more than two traffic tickets or warnings from police officers over the past two years.

8. I have taken or plan to take an older-driver improvement course.

9. I always wear my seat belt.

10. My car is serviced on a regular schedule.

Figure 5   Driver's Self-Assessment Questionnaire

Legally, the states have the final word over who can and cannot drive. Many states are passing legislation to help them identify the most dangerous drivers among the elderly. If a caregiver has a concern about the driving abilities of an elderly person, the state police can give information on the procedures for reexamination and on whether physicians are required to report potentially impaired patients to the state police.

Gadgets and Devices for Daily Living

In 1987, the Museum of Modern Art in New York City had an exhibit of commercially available products designed and developed to help people of all ages with disabilities live independently. Many of these products, such as recliners, whirlpool baths, contour beds, telephone volume controls, hand-held shower heads, and remote controls for appliances, have been mainstreamed for the general population. Since almost everyone develops some form of disability as the result of aging or accidents, many adaptive devices to help make our lives easier and allow us to maintain independence are being manufactured and marketed.

More than 13,000 commercially available aids and devices help with daily living tasks ranging from fastening zippers and pulling on clothes to getting around the house, using appliances and gadgets, driving cars, answering telephones, cooking, and shaving. Many are available from local medical supply houses and home-health catalogues. Other sources of information are listed at the end of this chapter. Consumers may also check the rehabilitation departments of hospitals and nursing homes or specialized rehabilitation centers and hospitals. Many national appliance, business machine, and utility companies have special needs departments that offer information and catalogues.

Some products are stocked in appliance or electronic equipment stores, telephone stores, and toy stores. Children's cassette recorders have large-print labels and easy-to-press buttons suited to the needs of the elderly. Telephone help lines offer knowledgeable information from specialists who have no affiliation with the companies that manufacture the products. Chapter 8 lists organizations that offer information on adaptive devices to help people affected by a specific disability, chronic illness, sensory impairment, or disease.

Telephone Reassurance Programs and Friendly Visitors

These programs are usually operated by volunteers and sponsored through neighborhood groups, local churches and synagogues, and social service organizations. Volunteers call or visit on a regular basis or on a schedule agreed on by the elderly person and the volunteer. These programs can be located through the local Area Agency on Aging or by contacting the sponsoring agency. The telephone book's section on Human Services lists these groups under several headings such as Aging or Volunteers. Public libraries often keep listings of such local services.

Identification and Medical Devices

Information on these devices can be obtained from medical supply houses, pharmacies, and some of the associations listed in Chapter 8 and books listed in Chapter 9. Medical identifications such as the medical alert necklace or bracelet give valuable medical information and the name and address of the wearer. These can be customized by the Medic Alert Foundation. Some pharmacies sell Medical Alert items with information on many typical medical problems.

Technology has generated inexpensive and practical items that can help older people maintain a relatively worry-free and safe life-style. A computerized watch can be programmed with stored vital medical data. When the medical emblem on the face of the watch is pressed, the stored medical information appears frame by frame in the illuminated watch display. A plastic card that fits in a wallet and resembles a credit card is available, showing the wearer's latest EKG and other medical information.

Personal Emergency Response Systems (PERS)

PERS, also called medical emergency response systems, are signaling devices that summon help to a residence during an emergency. PERS are simple electronic devices that send a call for help to someone who will be able to respond. PERS offer independence and a sense of security through a touch of a button. Each system has two parts. The first is a small transmitter (the portable help button) that the person wears or carries, and the second part is the console or receiving base connected to the user's telephone. For example, if the user falls or feels chest pains, he or she can summon immediate help by simply pressing the button on the transmitter. The system has an effective range of approximately 200 feet, which means a radio signal can be sent from almost anywhere in an average-size house to the console. When the help signal is received by the console, an automatic dialing device calls a preselected emergency telephone number. Most systems can dial out even if the phone is off the hook.

Almost all PERS are programmed to call an emergency response center where the source of each incoming call is electronically identified through special coding. The response center's staff quickly reviews the user's file, which contains medical history, list of medications, and the names and telephone numbers of people to be notified in case of an emergency, local emergency services, and other prerecorded information. The response center telephones the user or, with some systems, communicates through a speaker phone built into the console. If the user does not respond or the response center determines that an emergency exists, then a responder or an emergency service is alerted to go to the user's home. In most systems, PERS personnel will monitor the situation until the crisis is resolved.

PERS have been on the market for about 20 years, and there are many systems available. Consumers should research and evaluate the various PERS before choosing one. PERS can be rented, purchased, or leased. Some hospitals rent out PERS and also function as the response center. If a care receiver's doctor is on staff at a hospital that offers this service, then this is the logical system to look into first.

Some insurance policies cover the charges for a PERS, if the doctor recommends using one, but generally the consumer pays the charges. Some hospitals and social service agencies subsidize fees for low-income users. Medicare does not cover PERS costs. The overall cost depends on the type of equipment and additional features the user opts for, such as two-way radio capacity or auxiliary transmitters. Lease arrangements vary, and all contracts should be reviewed carefully and several models tested before a selection is made.

Drug Interactions

FACTS

- In 1982, 75.2 percent of noninstitutionalized people over 65 years old had at least one prescribed medication. The mean number of prescriptions acquired yearly by people over 65 was ten.

- Nonprescription or over-the-counter drugs are heavily used by people over 65. It is estimated that some people use up to ten over-the-counter medications.

Older people tend to see more than one doctor, take more prescription medications than younger patients, and have a variety of problems relating to the management of and compliance with their drug regimens. Studies have shown that many elderly people do not tell each doctor what the other doctors have prescribed; fail to get clear, understandable instructions on how to take their medications; and do not regard their over-the-counter drugs, vitamins, or home remedies as medications. Rarely do they consider the potential interactions of food and alcohol with their medications.

Adverse drug interactions in the elderly may produce lapses of memory, trouble thinking clearly, difficulty sleeping, or restlessness—all reactions that mimic the symptoms of Alzheimer's disease and other conditions that are thought of as part of the aging process. There are many potential problems—the elderly take more drugs, have a higher rate of noncompliance, are more susceptible to adverse drug reactions, and may not be eating properly. Further, they may be using outdated prescriptions or taking medications prescribed by different doctors that may cause an overdose, adversely interact, or cause an overly complex medication regimen. The medicines may not even be stored in the correct place.

An elderly patient should have one primary care doctor to evaluate and monitor medications. The elderly person should pay close attention to any significant physical or mental differences after starting a new medications. The change should not be dismissed as old age, stress, or fatigue. The doctor should be notified and the prescription and dosage evaluated. Many medications may not combine comfortably in the elderly person and could create adverse reactions that make the patient feel older and sicker, or may actually be dangerous to health.

Greater consultation between doctor and patient will help inform the patient about the effects of drug interaction and the importance of compliance with instructions. The patient and the caregiver need to ask:

1. What is the name of the drug, and what is it supposed to do?

2. How and when do I take it, and when do I stop using it?

3. What foods, drinks, other drugs, or activities should I avoid while taking this drug?

4. What are the side effects, and what should I do if they occur?

5. Is any written information available about this drug?

Patients and their caregivers need to take personal responsibility for knowing how medications and other drugs work alone and together, what reactions they should be aware of, and how the medications should be taken.

Safety, well-being, independence, and comfort are obtainable goals for the elderly. Many ideas, services, products, and guides are available to help the elderly and the caregiver achieve these goals. Adapting the home allows an elderly person to live longer independently and in the community.

References

Gary D. Branson. *The Complete Guide to Barrier-Free Housing: Convenient Living for the Elderly and the Physically Handicapped*. White Hall, VA: Betterway Publications, 1991.

Hartford Insurance Group, Community Affairs Department. *How To Modify a Home To Accommodate the Needs of an Older Adult: The Hartford House*. Hartford, CT: Hartford Insurance Group,

LaBuda, Dennis, ed. *The Gadget Book: Ingenious Devices for Easier Living. An AARP Book*. Glenview, IL: Scott, Foresman, 1985.

Malfetti, James L., and Darlene J. Winter. *Concerned about an Older Driver? A Guide for Families and Friends*. Washington, DC: AAA Foundation for Traffic Safety, 1991.

Malfetti, James L., and Darlene J. Winter. *Drivers 55 Plus: Test Your Own Performance: A Self-Rating Form of Questions, Facts, and Suggestions for Safe Driving*. Washington, DC: AAA Foundation for Traffic Safety, 1986.

Pfeiffer, George J. *Taking Care of Today and Tomorrow: A Resource Guide for Health, Aging, and Long-Term Care*. Reston, VA: Center for Corporate Health Promotion, 1989.

Pynoos, Jon, and Evelyn Cohen. *Home Safety Guide for Older People: Check It Out, Fix It Up*. Washington, DC: Serif Press, 1990.

Salmen, John P. S. *The Do Able Renewable House: Making Your Home Fit Your Needs*. Washington, DC: AARP, 1986.

U.S. Consumer Product Safety Commission. *Safety for Older Consumers: Home Safety Checklist*. Washington, DC: Government Printing Office, 1986.

Walser, Nancy. "When To Hang Up the Keys," *Harvard Health Letter* 17 (November 1991): 1–4.

Chapter 6

Housing Options

Introduction

Housing for the elderly is more than simply a structure made of a roof, brick, and mortar. A residence represents a way of living, a sense of independence, and security. As people age, physical and mental changes may necessitate a review of suitable housing options. Despite popular beliefs, to move or not to move is not the only question, and a nursing home is not the only solution.

Most older people prefer to remain in their own homes. Many times this is possible with additional supports. Chapter 3 discussed the various services that can be brought into the home. Older people also have the option of adapting the home to make it more comfortable and safer, as presented in Chapter 5. Adaptive equipment also can make performing daily activities easier. Yet, even with the various supports available, some older people cannot stay in the home because of declining health conditions or safety issues.

A number of living arrangements are available to older Americans. Aging people can select from a continuum of housing options designed to accommodate different financial situations, health conditions, and personal preferences. However, not every community offers all of the options discussed in this chapter, and some housing facilities have long waiting lists. Therefore, caregivers and older people are encouraged to discuss possible living arrangements in advance of a crisis or major illness.

This chapter discusses the various living arrangements available for older people by levels of dependency, provides insight into when a particular type of housing may be suitable, and lists consumer cautions.

FACTS

- Some 67 percent of non-institutionalized elderly people live with a spouse.

- About 30 percent of elderly people live alone.

- Older people change residence less often than do other age groups.

- About 55 percent of the elderly prefer to stay in their current homes for as long as possible.

- Only 5 percent of the elderly live in retirement communities or housing specifically built for the elderly.

- Approximately 20 percent of people living in senior housing view social activities as the aspect they like most about living with people over 60.

- Some 39 percent of elderly would prefer living in a senior citizens' building, if they lived in an apartment.

- Residents of congregate housing tend to be 75 years of age or older.

- Fees for assisted living facilities range from $240 to $2,500 per month.

Staying at Home

By far, older people prefer to age in place, i.e., to remain in their current housing for as long as possible. People feel comfortable in familiar surroundings. Many enjoy their current neighborhoods and are satisfied with knowing the neighbors, the best places to shop, and public transportation patterns.

Nonetheless, most homes and apartments do not accommodate the physical limitations that older people often experience. Stairs may be difficult to climb with arthritic legs, doorways may not be wide enough for walking devices, or bathrooms may pose safety hazards. Older homeowners may also find it physically difficult or too expensive to make repairs needed to improve safety as well as aesthetic concerns. Home adaptation and repair programs address these types of concerns and make it possible for some older people to continue living independently.

Home Adaptation Programs

Many older people can remain in their homes if modifications are made to maintain safety and compensate for the residents' diminishing physical capabilities. Most homes can be easily adapted to remove barriers, increase mobility, and meet specific needs of elderly residents. Following are some common housing adaptations identified in *Housing Options and Services for Older Adults*.

- Modify doorways to accommodate wheelchairs by replacing existing door hinges with swing-clear hinges, removing the doors, or replacing with sliding doors, pocket doors, or folding doors.

- Secure doormats and throw rugs to guard against dangerous falls.

- Replace standard doorknobs with levers for easy operation.

- Replace stairs that are too steep or narrow so that the risers are 6–7 inches high and treads are wide enough to allow the foot to rest comfortably.

- Add rounded handrails that extend beyond the top and bottom steps of stairs to provide support when negotiating steps.

- Place light switches at the tops and bottoms of stairways.

- Construct an outside ramp for wheelchairs.

- Replace faucets with levers for easy operation.

- Install grab bars next to toilets and in bathtubs and showers.

- Lower sinks to allow for easy use by wheelchair users.

- Raise and lower cabinets and countertops on adjustable brackets for easy access.

- Purchase a range with front or side control panels to eliminate reaching across heated areas.

- Purchase assistive devices that make daily activities easier to perform.

Home adaptations are useful for people who are experiencing some physical limitations yet are able to live independently. A physical or occupational therapist can often suggest useful adaptations as can certain disease-specific organizations such as the Muscular Dystrophy Association or the United Cerebral Palsy Society. State chapters of the American Institute of Architects also may be able to recommend specialists in home modification.

Home Repair

From time to time, all housing structures need repair and maintenance in order to eliminate health and safety hazards. Repairs such as insulation, minor plumbing, replacing rotted window frames, and repairing cracked sidewalks allow older homeowners to remain in a safe environment. However, necessary repairs may be overlooked by older homeowners on fixed incomes as too expensive.

Some communities have home repair programs, such as those provided by two federal programs, the Farmers Home Administration (FmHA) and the U.S. Department of Housing and Urban Development (HUD). FmHA provides low-interest loans and grants to older people in low-income households to bring their homes up to standard or to remove health hazards. HUD provides community development block grants for neighborhood revitalization. Many communities elect to offer home repair programs with block grant funds. In addition, state or area offices on aging may offer home repair programs for seniors. Older homeowners can also contact religious organizations, nonprofit community organizations, and the city or county department of housing and community development.

As home repair programs are not widely available, some older people will have to hire private contractors for home adaptation and repair. In doing so, homeowners should observe some cautions.

- Start by asking friends and family members to refer reliable contractors.

- Contact at least three potential contractors for any specific job.

- Request written bids and three references from each bidder.

- Carefully compare the costs, time estimates, and comments from references.

- Set up a schedule for payment that specifies who is to pay for raw materials.

- Check to see if the work being done requires a license or permit from any local government agency such as the office of consumer affairs.

Relocating

There are numerous reasons why older people move from their homes to another independent living arrangement. The neighborhood may have deteriorated over the years and become too noisy or unsafe. Friends, neighbors, and familiar places of businesses may have relocated outside of the neighborhood. The current home may be too large, expensive, or difficult to maintain. There may be too many structural barriers, or the older person may simply prefer to move closer to family and friends.

In general, seniors have a strong preference for remaining in familiar surroundings. They may feel an attachment to their own homes and to shops, friends, social and cultural centers, trusted doctors and medical facilities, and familiar transportation systems. For some, remaining in the current home is financially attractive if the mortgage is paid off or has a low balance. Rents may be very low because of the number of years in residence.

In deciding whether to relocate, understanding why the older person wants to move will help caregivers identify housing options to meet specific needs. Before deciding whether to relocate, caregivers and older people may want to ask:

- Is the current home affordable?
- Is the current home too large or difficult to maintain?

- Are there barriers in the home that make moving about burdensome?

- How important is being close to places of worship, stores, public transportation, and other familiar places?

- How important is being close to family and friends?

- How much money can the older person comfortably spend on housing?

- Is sharing a home with another person a possibility?

- Is an age-segregated neighborhood desired?

- Is personal safety and health monitoring a prerequisite?

- How important is the availability of organized recreation?

Answering these questions will help elders and caregivers decide on the type of independent living situation that will be most suitable and provide the right amount of independence and privacy. Older adults can also decide how much responsibility they desire for maintaining a household.

FACTS

- Some 22 percent of older Americans expect to move.

- Only 13 percent say they would really like to move.

- About 43 percent of older Americans have lived in their present homes for about 20 years.

- In 1989, only 17 percent had moved within the past five years.

- Approximately 63 percent of those who move stay in the same city or county.

Case Study

Approximately two months after Mrs. Johnson's husband died, she decided that her current house was too big and too empty. Mrs. Johnson's health was good but she did not want to continue maintaining such a large home. Besides, she felt that the home held too many memories of her late husband. She immediately sold her home and purchased a smaller one several miles away.

Mrs. Johnson was not happy in her new home. Her neighbors were much younger, shopping was less convenient, and the new house demanded as much time and money to maintain as the old one. She found that she still experienced emotional pain associated with bereavement.

Mrs. Johnson's situation is typical of a recently widowed person who moves in an attempt to escape feelings of loneliness and grief. Deciding to relocate under stressful situations such as the recent death of a spouse often leads to poor decision making. Older people are advised not to relocate until the many factors associated with moving are considered and the various options reviewed.

Housing Types

Moving into a Smaller House

Many seniors think moving to a smaller home will solve all their concerns. However, it is important to keep in mind that having a smaller home is the same as having a larger home, except that it is smaller. In other words, homeowners are responsible for all indoor and outside maintenance, taxes, water, sewerage, and trash collection, whatever the size of the home. They still receive the advantages of adequate space, tax benefits, and independence. Elders and their caregivers should consider whether a smaller home is affordable and whether it will be easy to maintain after several years.

Renting

Older people may find renting a good option. All types of housing are available for rent—homes, apartments, and single rooms. Renting allows the resident to leave the responsibility of maintenance to the owner and is less expensive than home ownership. However, rental property is usually smaller than a private home. Thus, the older person may need to discard furniture that does not fit in the new space.

Some property owners do not allow renters to have pets and may enforce other undesirable tenant rules. Neighbors may be noisy, unclean, or difficult. Older people considering renting should inspect the rental property thoroughly and review the leasing agreement carefully. Potential renters may want to visit the neighborhood during both daylight and evening hours before signing a lease.

Condominiums

Increasingly, condominiums are becoming the favorite housing choice of older people. Condominiums combine the tax benefits of home ownership with the convenience of renting. In condo living, the owner holds title to the living unit and shares ownership with other tenants in common areas—exterior walls, parking areas, walkways, grounds, and recreational facilities. Condo dwellers are responsible for mortgage and for condo fees, which are usually paid in monthly installments to maintain the common property. Owners belong to a condo association which governs the complex. People interested in condominium living should examine the condominium declaration and bylaws very carefully. These documents detail the terms of the sale and the rules under which the owners live.

Cooperatives (Co-ops)

Cooperatives, like condominiums, combine the benefits of home ownership with the convenience of renting. Housing co-ops are legal corporations whereby owners purchase shares of the corporation in order to live in a specific unit. Owners are required to cooperate in the ownership and management of the corporation. People buying into the co-op must pay a one-time membership fee and a monthly payment to cover a share of the mortgage, interest, and operating expenses for the building.

The most frequently cited concern about co-ops is the transfer of equity when a member leaves the co-op and sells the shares. Some co-ops allow members to sell their shares and equity for any price the market will bear. Others limit equity based on a certain percentage for each year of residency to keep the price of the co-op affordable. Another concern is that most cooperatives' bylaws give the corporation the right to refuse a buyer.

Shared Housing

In a shared housing situation, two or more people share common elements of a living unit yet reserve individual private sleeping quarters. These arrangements thereby reduce living expenses for each person participating. This type of arrangement can also help older people remain in their homes longer with companionship and security. A house sharer may assist an older homeowner with housework, personal care, chores, and companionship. It is important, however, to clarify expectations and responsibilities at the beginning of this type of arrangement.

In some communities, home-matching programs introduce potential roommates based on preferences, attitudes, and expectations. Potential house sharers are advised to examine their needs and expectations before considering this option. They must also screen potential roommates and ask for character references. Older people are cautioned to consider how home sharing will affect entitlements such as food stamps and Supplemental Security Income (SSI). Those thinking of sharing a home should consider these points:

- How much rent and utilities should each person pay?

- How will household chores be divided?

- Will each person have access to other parts of the house?

- What type of person would be suitable—sex, smoking and drinking habits, etc.?

- Are pets and visitors welcomed?

Accessory Apartments

For some elders, an accessory apartment may be an ideal living alternative. An accessory apartment is a completely private living unit within a single-family home. Accessory apartments are known by a number of names, including English basement, mother-daughter residence, and single-family conversion. Usually, the unit has all the features of a stand-alone apartment—kitchen, bathroom, sleeping area—and often a separate entrance.

Accessory apartments contribute to an increase in the homeowner's income and the sense of security of both parties. The arrangement is good for some adult children and their parents because it allows total privacy yet makes supports for the older person easily available when needed.

There are three primary precautions for people interested in accessory apartments. First, zoning may prohibit the creation of an accessory apartment. Homeowners should contact the local zoning agency for information on codes. When accessory arrangements are prohibited by codes, older homeowners may receive special permits or variances to create an accessory apartment. Second, the rental procedures for an accessory apartment are the same as for other rental property. Standard leases are available at the local library, and the local newspaper provides information on the going rates for rents. Third, tenants should be screened carefully.

Echo Housing

The rewards of echo housing are similar to those of accessory apartments for adults and their older relatives. Both provide privacy, closeness, and security. An echo house is a separate, private living unit temporarily installed on the side or in the backyard of the primary home. Echo houses, also known as granny flats, promote independence and mutual support between households. Echo houses usually cost between $17,000 and $25,000. They are generally produced as manufactured housing so that they are removable and reusable.

As with accessory apartments, many communities have zoning codes that prohibit the construction of echo houses for fear that the appearance of the neighborhood will be harmed. Homeowners sometimes may apply for special permits or variances to build an echo cottage.

Moving in with the Caregiver

When a caregiver notices a decline in an aging relative, a common reaction is to suggest that the relative move in with the caregiver's family. Care providers frequently believe that sharing a home will ensure that the older person's needs are met.

They presume that providing care will be easier because of close proximity.

Sharing a household with an older relative can be rewarding and can make providing care easier. However, several issues need to be considered before deciding to combine households.

- Does the older person really want to share a home with the caregiver?

- Where will the older person sleep?

- Must the older person share a bedroom, or will another family member be displaced?

- Will the older person have socialization opportunities in the new neighborhood?

- Is transportation available for medical and other appointments?

- How will other family members, including children, need to adjust their schedules to accommodate the older person?

- How will the family's finances be affected?

- What type of relationship exists between the older relative and other family members?

Retirement Communities

A retirement community is a self-contained residential complex for older people that emphasizes socialization and recreation. Retirement facilities may also provide minimal services to residents. These communities offer low-maintenance housing in a secure environment. A retirement community can be a high-rise building or an entire town. Residents may rent or own their homes.

Retirement communities are not suited for all elders. This type of housing arrangement can be fairly expensive, depending on the type of housing selected and the activities and services provided. In addition, some elderly people do not like to live in age-segregated communities. Others may not be interested in the recreational activities offered. People thinking of moving into a retirement community should consider the following questions:

- What are the current and projected costs of living in this community?

- How flexible is the community in adapting to residents' changing needs over time?

- What services are included in the monthly rate?

- How satisfied are other residents with the way the community is managed?

- What are the plans for renovations and repairs?

- Is the community secure?

- Is the older person willing to live within the rules of the community?

Congregate Housing

Congregate housing provides elderly and disabled people with shelter and limited services. Most congregate housing facilities are 50- to 150-unit apartment buildings or a single-story complex with special architectural features to accommodate older people. Residents of congregate housing do not need 24-hour supervision or care.

Although congregate housing varies from location to location, facilities typically provide separate living quarters, meals served in a common dining area, and social activities. Some congregate facilities offer additional services, such as health monitoring, and social and recreational activities. Others make housekeeping and transportation services available. Some congregate facilities offer an extensive array of services by employing social workers, activities personnel, and health professionals such as a nurse or a podiatrist.

Monthly charges for congregate housing facilities vary and depend upon the location and the services offered. The American Association of Retired Persons (AARP) estimates that single people pay between $600 and $1,500 a month and couples pay $800 to $2,000 a month. Some congregate housing was constructed with funds from the HUD Section 8 program, a rent-supplement program that allows participants to pay one-third of their income toward rent while the government pays the balance.

Other congregate facilities were built with Section 202 funds from HUD to serve low-income individuals, and private organizations also build and operate congregate facilities.

Before moving into a congregate housing unit, consumers are encouraged to visit several potential sites, take a tour, talk to residents, and stay for a meal or even overnight. Ask to review a copy of the lease and a list of services included in the basic fee. Also ask to review a copy of the facility's policies and rules before signing a lease.

Multiple-Level Living

Multiple-level living offers two or more levels of care in the same residential facility. Thus, a person can remain in the same environment even if his or her health improves or deteriorates. This option avoids the need to transfer an older person from setting to setting in order to receive the level of health care required.

Continuing Care Retirement Communities (CCRC)

CCRCs, sometimes referred to as life-care communities, offer a life-care contract assuring the level of care needed until death. As dependence increases, CCRCs allow residents to continue to use recreational facilities, personal care, services, and medical care within the same setting. CCRCs may offer apartments, condominiums, or single-family homes. The actual services offered by CCRCs vary greatly from location to location. Typically, however, they offer a continuum of supportive services and health care. Most residents are active, involved elderly people who desire recreational activities as well as an array of social supports. CCRCs are not appropriate for people with insufficient income or people needing skilled care upon entrance into the community.

CCRC contracts fall into several categories:

Fee-for-services   Fees cover services and amenities except long-term skilled care. If skilled care is available, it requires additional fees.

Modified   Fees cover services, amenities, and a limited
amount of skilled care. If a resident needs more than
the specified amount of skilled care, additional charges
are made.
Extensive   Fees cover services and amenities including
long-term skilled care.

Naturally, contracts offering more extensive services are more
expensive. Residents of CCRCs pay a one-time entrance fee
that can be nonrefundable or partially refundable and monthly
fees. On average, entrance fees are approximately $50,000 and
monthly fees average close to $850. In addition, some facilities
require residents to have Medicare Part A and Part B and private
insurance to help defray operating costs.

Although the federal government does not regulate CCRCs,
35 states have consumer-protection laws that cover them. Regulations vary from state to state but they generally require CCRCs
to disclose financial records and information about operations
and ownership. Different agencies within each state are responsible for monitoring CCRCs, and the Continuing Care Accreditation Commission accredits CCRCs.

Over the past several years, some CCRCs have experienced
severe problems. More than 10 percent have gone bankrupt, and
some have raised monthly fees in order to remain solvent, causing residents to be priced out of the community. Consequently,
consumers are encouraged to address the following issues when
considering CCRCs:

- Identify the older person's needs and preferences as a basis
  for selecting a suitable community.

- Talk with the state agency responsible for regulating
  CCRCs.

- Contact several facilities and ask for a introductory packet,
  a copy of the contract, the resident's handbook, and
  financial reports.

- Visit several sites that can meet the identified needs, and
  talk with the residents, staff, and residents' council.

- Find out how monthly fees are adjusted and how often fees have been adjusted in the past.

- Have an attorney review and compare contracts from communities that interest you.

- Have a financial advisor review financial records.

- Explore background information on the owners and operators.

- Examine vacancy rates and inquire how these rates affect the financial security of the community.

Assisted Living Facilities

Assisted living facilities (ALFs) are known by many different names—boarding care homes, congregate residential facilities, domiciliaries, sheltered care facilities, and foster homes. ALFs serve older people who need 24-hour supervision and offer an extensive array of supportive services. Although facilities vary in style and size, residents typically are provided a room, three meals per day, assistance with personal care, laundry services, transportation, and medication supervision. Some assisted living facilities also arrange for residents to receive senior services in the community such as adult day care, transportation, and congregate meals.

ALFs have frequently been referred to as a regulatory jungle. Although all states license ALFs, licensing requirements vary from state to state. To complicate matters further, ALFs fall under the jurisdiction of several state, county, and city agencies that frequently have inconsistent requirements regarding safety, health, and zoning. The state's long-term care ombudsman who is responsible for handling consumer complaints can help potential residents and caregivers identify licensed ALFs.

Monthly fees for assisted living facilities vary greatly, averaging $240 to $2,500 per month. In some states, residents are eligible for subsidies through Medicaid, HUD Section 8, and state subsidy programs. Consumers are encouraged to be sure what services are covered by the basic fee. *A Home Away from Home: Consumer Information on Board and Care Homes* suggests that consumers ask these questions before selecting a facility:

- Are the house rules compatible with the older person's life-style?

- Is the facility conveniently located to public transportation, shops, and places of worship?

- Are safety measures in place such as sprinklers, smoke detectors, and handrails?

- Who are the staff members, and what are their qualifications and training?

- Is the food served nutritious, appetizing, and prepared according to dietary restrictions?

- Are residents provided with a written service plan that is reviewed and adjusted periodically?

- Does the facility follow sound financial management practices?

- How satisfied are current residents?

Nursing Facilities

As the name implies, nursing facilities, or nursing homes, provide residents with nursing care 24 hours per day. People needing constant medical care or supervision will find that nursing homes deliver the care needed. Typically, nursing homes offer three levels of care. Custodial care includes supervision and non-medical personal services such as bathing, dressing, and grooming. Intermediate care is basic nursing care and is best suited for people with long-term chronic illnesses and limitations. Skilled care means medical services prescribed by a physician including rehabilitative therapies.

FACTS

- At any given time, 5 percent of older Americans reside in a nursing home.

- About 43 percent of the elderly who turned 65 in 1990 will enter a nursing home before they die.

- Approximately 75 percent of nursing home residents are women.

Nursing homes cost between $25,000 and $52,000 per year, depending upon geographic location. In 1989, residents and families paid for 45 percent of nursing home charges. Medicaid, the state-federal health insurance program for low-income and medically needy people, paid 43 percent of the bill. Medicare, federal health insurance for older people, paid about 2 percent, and private, long-term care insurance paid 1 percent.

Nursing facilities are licensed by the state, but state licensing is not an indicator of quality. State officials conduct unannounced inspections at least once every 15 months and, on average, every 12 months. Inspectors investigate how well nursing facilities meet minimal standards for fire protection, fiscal management, nutrition services, and building maintenance. Inspections also assure that facilities meet the conditions for participating in the Medicare and Medicaid programs. Some homes elect to undergo more extensive inspections by becoming accredited by groups like the Joint Commission on Accreditation of Healthcare Organizations. Accreditation is often viewed as the Good Housekeeping seal of approval.

Over the past several years, the nursing home industry has received much negative publicity regarding patient care. However, the first comprehensive nursing home reform law, the Omnibus Budget Reconciliation Act (OBRA) of 1987, is currently being enforced. This federal legislation increased standards in the areas of residents' rights, nurse aide training, inspection of nursing homes, staffing, and enforcement of regulations. Among other things, OBRA 1987:

- Increased residents' rights to be informed about and participate in care planning, have their property respected, inhibit inappropriate discharges, and have records and mail maintained in a confidential manner.

- Provided opportunities for residents to participate in the inspection process.

- Required that nurse aides complete a competency-based training program.

- Assured appropriate placement of mentally retarded and mentally ill residents through preadmission screening and annual resident review (PASAAR).

- Required 24-hour coverage by licensed nurses.

- Increased sanctions for noncompliance to include denial of payments, fines, and appointment of temporary management.

The decision to move into a nursing facility is often a difficult one. Many older people feel that a nursing home is one step from the grave. Families often feel guilty about putting the older person in a home. For all involved, many questions, feelings, and apprehensions are associated with nursing home placement.

Decisions regarding nursing home placement are often made during a crisis situation when there are few facilities from which to choose. A sudden illness or accident can necessitate the need for a nursing home at a time when no one is prepared to make an intelligent decision. But older people and their families can plan ahead in order to select a facility that best meets the needs and preferences of the elderly person. Chapter 7 contains further details on nursing home selection, placement, and financing.

References

American Association of Retired Persons (AARP). *Congregate Housing Factsheet.* Washington, DC: AARP, 1991.

AARP. *Continuing Care Retirement Communities Factsheet.* Washington, DC: AARP, 1991.

AARP. *Factsheet, Long-Term Care.* Washington, DC: AARP, 1991.

AARP. *Housing Options for Older Americans.* Washington, DC: AARP, 1985.

AARP. *A Profile of Older Americans 1990.* Washington, DC: AARP, 1990.

AARP. *Understanding Senior Housing for the 1990s.* Washington, DC: AARP, 1990.

Edelman, Toby S. "The Nursing Home Reform Law: Issues for Litigation," *Clearinghouse Review* 24, no. 6 (1990): 545–549.

Gillespie, Ann E., and Katrinka Smith. *Housing Options and Services for Older Adults.* Choices and Challenges. Santa Barbara, CA: ABC-CLIO, 1990.

Haske, Margaret. *A Home Away From Home: Consumer Information on Board and Care Homes.* Washington, DC: AARP, 1988.

Horne, Jo. *The Nursing Home Handbook: A Guide for Families.* Glenview, IL: Scott, Foresman, 1989.

Kemper, P., and Christopher M. Murtaugh. *Lifetime Use of Nursing Home Care.* 324, no. 9 Washington, DC: U.S. Agency for Health Care Policy and Research, Public Health Service, Department of Health and Human Services, February 28, 1991.

Matthews, Joseph. *Eldercare: Choosing and Financing Long-Term Care.* Berkeley, CA: Nolo Press, 1990.

National Consumer Law Center. *Life-Care Contracts: Retirement without Risk? Senior Consumer Alert: A Special Bulletin for Complaint Handlers.* Washington, DC: AARP, 1986.

Chapter 7

Nursing Home Placement

Introduction

Nursing home placement is one of the most difficult decisions that a caregiver has to make, regardless of the relationship to the older person—spouse, child, other family member, or friend. This decision has been found to be more stressful and to create more grief than the actual death of the care receiver.

The very term *nursing home* brings shudders to most people and conjures up negative images. To many people, the term suggests impersonality, regimentation, failure, and abandonment. This negative impression is reinforced by the media's sensationalistic highlighting of mistreatment, abuse, loneliness, and neglect, all within an environment of uncaring people in an unclean institution. Although these images may describe some nursing homes, most nursing homes are between the extremes of very bad and very good.

This chapter deals with finding a nursing home, making the best decision, implementing the decision as comfortably as possible for the elderly person, and becoming an effective caregiver after the move to a nursing home.

FACTS

- At any one time it is estimated that less than 5 percent of the population 65 or older is living in a nursing home.

- Of Americans 65 to 74, about 1 percent live in nursing homes, compared with 22 percent of those 85 or older.

- About 25 percent of the elderly will spend time in a nursing home, some for a short stay to recover from an operation or an illness, and some permanently because of dementia, chronic illness, or other problems that require continual nursing care or supervision.

- There are about 20,000 nursing homes in this country, serving about 5 percent of the older population.

Case Study

Mr. Green was living with his daughter, son-in-law, and granddaughter. He had macular degeneration, cancer of the spine, severe arthritis which made his hands gnarled and made walking very tiring, and a multitude of other illnesses. He insisted on staying alone in the house when the family left for work. His daughter left sandwiches and a thermos of beverage for his lunch. He had a portable phone attached to his wheelchair and listened to the TV when alone.

Mr. Green's mind never failed him, and he kept his sense of humor and a strong belief that he was not a burden to his family. After one of his many hospital stays his daughter insisted on having aides come in while she was working to make sure he was safe, that he ate, and that all his needs were attended to. This was a difficult decision for Mr. Green to accept, since he wanted to maintain his feeling of independence, but he agreed just to relieve his daughter's anxiety, "to make her feel better," as he put it.

His health deteriorated further, and soon Mr. Green needed care during the night and nursing care instead of aides during the day. The entire household was rearranged to accommodate his increasing disabilities. After he experienced a number of falls and his cancer spread, he went into the hospital and from there into a nursing home. This time the doctor told the family this would be a permanent arrangement since Mr. Green's health had worsened and so had the daughter's. From the doctor's viewpoint the daughter needed time off for rest and recuperation.

This family tried to maintain the elderly person in the home past the time when the family members were able to provide adequate health care. The primary caregiver almost reached the breaking point. Fortunately in this case, the father remained alert and reasonable, and the family could openly discuss the need for the nursing home.

There is no perfect nursing home, just as there is no perfect family. No nursing home can perform miracles by making the elderly, infirm person feel young and healthy, nor can it make the elderly person and the caregiver suddenly become friendly, pleasant, relaxed, and open with one another. Elderly residents are likely to experience problems in adjusting to living in a place that isn't their own home. The caregivers' role changes, as they become visitors.

Nursing home residents lose a great deal—independence, privacy, freedom of movement, and decision-making power, and they resent the nursing home, even if they had lost many of these rights and privileges before moving into the nursing home. There can be friction between residents as they face a difficult adjustment to the stresses of communal living while also coping with failing health, chronic pain, and a sense of being useless and abandoned. Residents may not like the food, the staff, the activities, the medical staff, the therapists, or the beauticians. Many residents constantly ask, When can I go home?

Most nursing homes do their best to make residents comfortable. The staff is sensitive to friction between roommates and tries to eliminate difficult, stress-provoking situations. Nursing homes give care, concern, and attention, many times with limited staff, limited resources, and the daily stresses of working with a population that has many medical and emotional problems. The nursing home staff also must deal with the family and friends of the residents, who can be as difficult in their own ways as the residents.

Caregivers trying to make the difficult decision about nursing home placement face an often overwhelming and frightening process of visiting nursing homes and selecting one. Most people do not know where to begin, what questions to ask, what to look for, and what types of nursing homes are available. If the nursing home decision must be made suddenly because of a crisis, the anxiety and stress levels are even higher. Many caregivers prefer to spare themselves this anxiety and refuse to think about it, saying that such a so-called disaster will never occur.

But the odds are not good enough for caregivers, particularly those caring for frail or chronically ill elderly people, to adopt an ostrich-like attitude. Caregivers who have investigated nursing homes as part of their overall caregiver preparation and planning strategy are better able to make a sound decision, especially if the need for a nursing home arises suddenly.

Planning should include analyzing the preferences and attitudes of the care receiver. The care receiver needs to be involved in each step of the decision and, if still mentally capable, have the ultimate right to make the final choice. Hasty, unilateral decisions made when the elderly person is alert can cause a disastrous nursing home placement. The elderly person can feel bewildered, coerced, treated as an infant, rejected, and resentful toward the caregiver and others involved in the placement process. Caregivers and care receivers also need sufficient time to prepare themselves emotionally for the change of residence. Deciding on nursing home placement often stirs up feelings of guilt, abandonment, betrayal, and failure, sometimes so intense that counseling may be helpful for everyone involved.

Determining Whether Nursing Home Placement Is Needed

The time to consider nursing home placement varies with each case, and for some the question never arises. But when such a decision becomes necessary, it is usually because of a combination of factors. There may be a severe disability that requires continual nursing care, or there may be partial disability and inadequate help in the home for care. Both of these situations may be paired with other reasons.

1. Alternatives such as foster care, personal care homes, or other assisted living arrangements have been ruled out because they do not offer the level of nursing care that is needed.

2. The physical and emotional demands on the caregiver have become too great.

3. The care receiver is becoming more difficult to cope with or increasingly demanding and uncooperative.

4. The caregiver is feeling too much stress from other problems such as family discord, marital strains, or financial difficulties.

When considering whether or not to place an older person in a nursing home, caregivers and care receivers should consider these questions:

1. Has the home been turned into a mini-hospital?

2. Is the caregiver on duty 24 hours a day?

3. Does the caregiver feel that there is no difference between night and day?

4. Are other conflicts or emotional problems within the household creating additional stresses and competing for the attention and time of the caregiver?

5. What will happen to the care receiver if the primary caregiver becomes overworked, stressed out, and sick? Who will step in? Is there another person to assume the caregiving responsibility?

Nursing homes are for chronically ill people, those with disabling dementia, and people recuperating from an illness or operation who need regular nursing care and other health services but do not need to be hospitalized. Nursing homes exist to help those people who need them, offer them a secure and safe environment, and provide continuous health care. For many families, the choice of a nursing home becomes appropriate when the elderly person's needs are very great, when there are no community options, and when all the attention and energy of the caregiver is focused on the care receiver. This situation can create two patients in need of care instead of only one.

Nursing Home Care Options

Nursing homes are considered by gerontologists to be total institutions because all of a resident's daily activities occur within the institution. While the staff members, physicians, medical technicians, volunteers, and visitors come and go, the resident stays in the same place for all daily activities and services. The nursing home staff determines the activities and policies. The residents therefore have very little control over daily activities that most people take for granted, such as when to eat, take a bath, or go to bed. There are two general types of nursing homes, nursing facilities and custodial care facilities, and they vary by the level of medical services they provide.

Nursing Facilities

Nursing facilities (NFs) provide around-the-clock supervision and treatment by a registered nurse under the direction of a doctor. NFs serve people who require continual medical services. The caregiver should make sure that any nursing facility being considered is certified by Medicare and Medicaid. Medicaid pays for care in a nursing facility for those who qualify, and Medicare pays for up to 100 days per benefit period under limited circumstances only in certified skilled nursing facilities (SNFs).

Custodial Care Facilities

Custodial care, or assisted living facilities provide group living for those who need supervision but not medical care. Personal assistance in the activities of daily living, such as help in eating, getting out of bed, bathing, dressing, and toileting is provided, along with supervision in taking medications. This level of care does not require the services of people with professional medical skills or training. Medicare does not pay for this type of care, but Medicaid does in some states.

Discussing the Nursing Home Option

Many elderly people are not alert enough to understand the rationale for the nursing home. Even when they understand the needs, they may become angry, resentful, uncooperative, and manipulative—laying a guilt trip on the caregiver. Trying to discuss the nursing home option can elicit one or more of these reactions. This response makes an upsetting decision and process more so, even when the caregiver realizes that this is the correct way to ensure care, comfort, and safety for the elderly person.

Aside from having to discuss this option with the elder, the caregiver must make the decision and feel comfortable with it.

Caregivers have to be fair and honest with themselves and their families in answering several questions.

1. Am I resisting nursing home placement because I feel guilty about not being able to continue giving care?

2. Do I feel that in some way I am shirking my duty or my responsibilities?

3. Am I concerned about what others will think of me for doing this?

4. Am I able to remain calm, unperturbed, and on top of all caregiving responsibilities?

5. Is the family life being affected? Is my relationship with the care receiver being affected? How about my social life and my work?

6. Can I continue to give all the care that is required?

7. Am I feeling resentful and angry? Am I communicating negative feelings to everyone around me, especially to the care receiver?

8. Am I looking at the situation through my eyes, thinking that I wouldn't want to live in a nursing home? Or am I able to view the nursing home as if I were the care receiver and say, This place has round-the-clock attendants. I can get care and help any time I need it. There are people to talk to, and I won't be alone any time.

The prospect of moving an elderly person from the home setting into a nursing home, even if it is understood intellectually to be best for the person's health, safety, and care, is still a painful emotional experience for everyone involved. It is important to understand why this decision is being made and to plan carefully before discussing the decision with the elderly person. If necessary, caregivers can role-play the proposed conversation with others before approaching the elderly person. They should be aware of and understand the emotional responses and reactions the care receiver may have. In role-playing, they can explore their own feelings and learn to respond sympathetically, calmly, and honestly to the reactions of the elderly person.

If there is no immediate crisis, but a caregiver can foresee that the elderly person will need the type of care that a nursing home offers, then raise the issue of nursing home care gradually over a period of time. Give the person time to think about it, visit several nursing homes together, and include the elderly person in all evaluations and discussions. Be prepared for expressions of anger, frustration, fear, and refusal to think of a nursing home as a possibility. It is important to allow enough time for the elderly person to think about the issues of the nursing home and to respond and express his or her feelings.

If the elderly person is aware of what is going on, even with a form of dementia, then the person should not be misled about nursing home placement. Telling an elderly person that it is for only a short stay, when everyone else involved knows that it is permanent, creates more problems. The caregiver feels guilty over both the deception and the placement. Failure to speak directly, honestly, and undefensively can lay the groundwork for continual strife, a poor relationship, and further mistrust.

The caregiver may admire the care receiver's determination to be independent, maintain control, and live among family and cherished possessions, and at the same time realize that the move to a nursing home is necessary. Once the decision is made, it is important to help the elderly person make the move without losing self-esteem or a sense of identity. The caregiver has to feel comfortable with what is being said to the elderly person and to emphasize that adaptation does not mean resignation or becoming lifeless and depressed. Adaptation means that as adults both are recognizing the realities of the situation and handling the emotional reactions to it. Caregivers and care receivers can work together to find ways to keep up the care receiver's interests and self-esteem. Caregivers must be prepared to listen in a nonjudgmental manner to the care receiver's complaints and feelings of anger, frustration, and abandonment. These suggestions will help in the discussion of nursing homes with the care receiver:

1. Include the care receiver and all who are involved in the care from the very beginning. Doing it all on your own may be easier in the beginning but it will cause

barriers in the development of trust and acceptance of changes.

2. Be truthful and specific. Being misled decreases trust and makes the truth more painful when it is learned after the fact. Be very specific when discussing the reasons why a nursing home placement is necessary: "Your arthritic condition and emphysema really need continual nursing care." Or: "You are forgetting to take your medications, and the doctors have noticed that this is causing several problems. Your blood sugar is not stabilized now, and other organs are becoming involved. You need professional monitoring on an ongoing basis." Or: "It is not safe for you to be here. You forget to turn off the stove, and a fire could start, and you and others could be badly injured."

3. Be reassuring but honest. You can help the care receiver by giving continual reassurance that you are not abandoning him or her, that you feel that the decision is the right one, and that you will maintain frequent contact. Do not paint an unrealistically rosy picture or say that the care receiver has nothing to worry about and that everything will be wonderful. Reassure the elderly person that you will listen, handle complaints, and be involved in care.

4. Promise only what you can really do. Be realistic about how often you will visit, who may come with you, and when you will bring the care receiver home for holidays or other visits. It is better to promise less and then be able to do more. Let the care receiver know what your limitations are.

5. Talk openly about feelings of guilt, obligation, and other uncomfortable topics. Acknowledge the care receiver's feelings and never deny them. If these suggestions make you feel uncomfortable or you think the care receiver will feel this way, then consider asking for professional help.

Locating and Evaluating a Nursing Home

An elderly person's primary care doctor may suggest to the caregiver that a nursing home is needed. The doctor may be able to suggest one or more nursing homes in the area to consider. The doctor probably understands both the care receiver's condition and that of the primary caregiver and recommends a nursing home based on concern for both.

While many doctors are knowledgeable about nursing homes and want the best for their patients, it is important to go beyond the doctor's recommendations. Some doctors become financially or professionally involved with nursing homes, and this may influence their recommendations. Some doctors do not have adequate information about the nursing homes in their area or know which ones would be the most appropriate. As a consumer for a nursing home, the primary caregiver needs to get many suggestions, do research, and conduct on-site investigations.

If a nursing home must be found quickly, the caregiver may have to accept whichever home has an available bed. The hospital's social service department or discharge planner can help the caregiver find a nursing home, offer suggestions, and contact the nursing home directly to make the transfer arrangements. Even with only a few days' notice, the caregiver should visit the recommended nursing homes and check some of the books mentioned in the Reference section at the end of this chapter.

When there is time to plan, caregivers should contact the local Area Agency on Aging and ask for a list of accredited nursing homes in the area. These lists are kept up-to-date and have pertinent information.

1. Number of beds available, and the number for Medicare or Medicaid patients
2. Range of services: rehabilitative, restorative, pharmaceutical, dietary, laboratory, radiology, mental health, and physical, occupational, and speech therapies
3. Type of licenses
4. Levels of care: skilled nursing, intermediate care, or custodial care
5. Costs

The yellow pages listing under Nursing Homes indicates which homes are conveniently located, but this should not be the only basis for selection. Published directories, such as those listed in Chapter 9, can be found in public libraries. This material will help caregivers understand what to ask and what to look for.

When reading published material, always check the date of publication. If you find a nursing home that interests you, call and ask for current information. Some areas have nursing home placement or information and referral services that can aid in the evaluation and selection of an appropriate nursing home. Fees for this service vary. Families of nursing home residents can also share their opinions. Other sources include family services associated with religious affiliations.

After you have established what to look for, visit the selected nursing homes and take along a checklist and questions for each nursing home. Do not rely on your memory or the nursing home's brochure. Make more than one visit to the nursing homes that you are considering at different times of the day. Ask to have a meal with the residents, preferably at midday, which is usually when the large meal of the day is served.

Speak with some residents, but make allowances for infirmities and dementia. Speak with residents' families and other visitors. If the nursing home has a family night program, a caregivers' support group, or other activities for the residents' caregivers and families, ask to attend one and get a sense of how the caregivers feel about the facility. You will also be able to observe how the professional staff interacts with caregivers and family members at these activities.

Ask to observe an activity group and check the monthly calendar to find out what type of activities are planned and how often. Notice whether the residents look well-cared for, clean, and well-dressed, making allowances for medical conditions. Watch how the staff talks to and interacts with the residents. Notice a range of staff members—nurses, aides, maintenance personnel, social workers, activities director, other professionals, and administrators.

Whether the nursing home search must be done quickly or is part of a planning program, the caregiver should contact the local nursing home ombudsman office for information. Many Area Agency on Aging offices have such an ombudsman, and states have them as part of the department on aging. Many large cities have a nursing home hotline. From these contacts, the caregiver can gather information about the reputation of the nursing home, how the professional community views it, and its overall history and track record.

The Entry Interview

After a nursing home has been selected, an entry interview will be scheduled, primarily for the nursing home to gather information about the resident, and for the caregiver and elderly person to learn about the home. For an efficient and productive interview, the caregiver and elderly person (if able to participate) should be prepared with a list of their own questions along with the information required by the nursing home. See Figure 6, Questions in a Nursing Home Entry Interview, for a list of questions that may be asked of the elderly person. Many of these questions may seem personal and unnecessary, but the information can be very useful to the staff in helping the elderly person adjust. Asking these questions is a good indication that the nursing home is interested in the elderly person as an individual.

Caregivers should also expect that the interview will include questions about funeral arrangements and preferences. From the nursing home's point of view, it is best to know in advance and not have to get this information at a time of crisis. The nursing home is interested in being prepared to carry out the resident's and the caregiver's wishes at the time of death.

The caregiver and elderly person will find it helpful to write down any pertinent information they learn in the interview. The law requires that the nursing home supply certain documents to a new resident.

Residents' bill of rights

Licensing certificates including nursing home administrator license

State nursing home license

Background Information on the Elderly Person

1. Name
2. Date of birth, place of birth
3. Marital status
4. Social Security number and Medicare number
5. What family members or friends should be contacted in case of an emergency?
6. Name, address, and telephone number of the primary care doctor
7. Do you wish to retain this doctor after nursing home placement? Is the doctor on staff at the nursing home?
8. Which hospital is preferred if one is needed?

Medical History of the Elderly Person

1. Height, weight
2. General physical condition
3. Current illnesses (bring a list and identify the most serious ones, including date of onset)
4. Immediate reason for considering the nursing home
5. Any recent hospitalization? If yes, where and for what reason?
6. Mobility, walking ability—alone, with a walker
7. Incontinency, bowel or bladder problems
8. Any psychological disturbances, such as chronic depression
9. Are there any recurrent behavioral problems such as abusive or violent behavior, alcoholism, or drug addiction?
10. Allergies or sensitivity to any medications?
11. List of prescription medications, prescribing doctor, and pharmacists
12. List of over-the-counter drugs currently being taken
13. Any special dietary needs or preferences?

Financial Considerations of the Elderly Person

1. Monthly income from pensions, savings, Social Security
2. Any current outstanding debts
3. Does the person own a home? If yes, what is the value?
4. Does a family member live in the house and plan to continue living there?
5. Is any other real estate owned by the elderly person?

Figure 6   Questions in a Nursing Home Entry Interview

Figure 6 (continued)

6. Assets such as stocks or savings
7. Are assets available for nursing home costs?
8. Who is responsible for managing the elderly person's financial affairs?

Personal Considerations

1. Religious background
2. Recreational and leisure interests
3. Other social or psychological information that would be helpful for the staff to know.

American Association of Homes for the Aging certificate

American Nursing Home Association certificate

Joint Committee on Accreditation of Hospital certificate (in some homes)

Copy of the state survey that nursing homes certified for Medicare and Medicaid must prepare every year

Moving-in Day

Before the actual moving-in day, arrange to fix up the elderly person's new room with personal mementos, family photos, other pictures, wall plaques, knickknacks, a favorite chair, or other items that will help make the room more personal and familiar for the care receiver. If the nursing home allows residents to bring their own furniture, have this ready to be moved in on the same day or before the care receiver moves in. The timing of these arrangements depends on where the care receiver is coming from—the hospital, the caregiver's home, the care receiver's home or apartment, or another facility such as a personal care home. Other items that may fit into the relatively small space of a nursing home room and bring happy and pleasant memories to the care receiver may include a personal TV set, radio, clock, reading lamp, plants (blooming plants are especially cheerful), photograph albums, hobby materials, books, and corkboard for displaying pictures, notes, and artwork from grandchildren.

A laundry hamper for personal laundry, good plastic hangers for clothing, nice paper for lining the shelves, and plastic containers for folded clothing (if the care receiver has used them) are also useful. Make sure that everything is labeled, even the hangers. A laundry pen, preferably with black ink, is very good for labeling personal items, including walkers, canes, and other assistive devices. Personal items such as dentures, hearing aids, and reading glasses should be labeled by inscribing or etching the person's name or Social Security number. Remember that glasses and dentures can be easily lost and difficult to identify and replace.

On the actual moving-in day, it is important for family members and friends to be available all day to give emotional support and help the care receiver settle in. It is helpful to have several people involved so that while some people are putting away clothing or filling out forms, the others can stay with the elderly person.

Caregiving after Nursing Home Placement

Both the care receiver and the caregiver may feel that nursing home placement inevitably signifies the end of life, relationships, caring, and involvement. In reality, a lot of living and caring goes on in a nursing home. The caregiver's concern and care do not change; the environment in which it is given and the amount of time that is given are the things that change.

By becoming effective visitors to a nursing home resident, caregivers and others can reassure the elderly person and themselves that there has been no abandonment. When the caregivers are relieved of providing functional care, such as feeding, dressing, and administering medications, and relieved of the worry about safety, coordinating schedules, and being pulled in all directions, then they can fulfill a new caregiving role. As effective visitors, they can be the link to the outside world, family members, and friends, and the elderly person's ombudsman, in addition to continuing their personal emotional relationship.

The primary caregiver may be reluctant to give up the functional care and other services for the care receiver. These tasks and services are now the responsibility of the nursing home staff. The primary caregiver is responsible for the very important, personal things that only those closest to the resident can perform. Caregivers can make the visit a satisfying time for the resident, observe the resident's needs, and supply items that will help maintain the elderly person's life-style and interests, as much as health and mental condition allow. With the permission of the professional staff, visitors can supplement the nursing home's menu with familiar foods and beverages, help with letter writing, share the observance of religious occasions, and bring in things from the outside world that have meaning. The primary caregiver and other visitors become the eyes and ears of the outside world for the nursing home resident.

Caregivers can also watch for subtle physical and mental changes, such as declining appetite, deterioration of vision and hearing, apathy, and sadness. These changes should be reported to the nursing home staff. The caregiver advocates for the resident, listening to complaints, reviewing them with the appropriate staff, and deciding whether action is justified or whether the elderly person misunderstood or is seeking attention. Making the visit count creates a vital link between the resident and the family, the resident and the community, and the resident and the nursing home staff. In effect it is a link with life.

How Often Should the Caregiver Visit?

A caregiver should visit a nursing home resident often enough to maintain the relationship but not so often that it interferes with the resident's integration into the nursing home's routine and community. If the visits are too frequent, a resident may decline to take part in activities, not try to make friends with other residents, or refuse assistance from the staff and instead wait for the caregiver.

The caregiver may experience some difficulties in adjusting to the role of visitor. The very word sounds formal and is not descriptive of the relationship. The nursing home is a strange, unfamiliar place to both caregiver and care receiver. The visits may be interrupted by the staff because of the nursing and medication schedule. And there are different smells and sounds.

The caregiver sees sick and debilitated people and may think, "this is not want I want for my future." Caregivers are reminded of their own mortality and the possibility of becoming sick and dependent. They may feel angry at the care recipient for becoming dependent, for needing the nursing home, and for the loss of the relationship and the way things were. The adjustment involves a grieving process, and the caregiver may want to get help from the social worker in the nursing home, from another professional, or from a support group.

When deciding how often to visit, these questions should be reviewed:

1. How often did I see this person before nursing home admission?

2. How much of that was "quality time," how much was spent in giving care, and how much of that time did I resent giving?

3. What are the demands of my daily schedule?

4. How often do I feel I should visit? And why do I feel I should visit?

5. How often do others feel I should visit? Why do they feel this?

6. How can I resolve conflict between my view and others' opinions about the frequency of visits?

The length of visiting time is determined by balancing the best interests of the resident against those of the visitor. As the resident's condition changes, the visiting schedule should be reassessed. When a resident is forgetful or confused or both, shorter and more frequent visits may be more productive and appropriate.

Where Should the Caregiver Visit?

If the resident is not bedridden, it is better to circulate around the nursing home through the common areas such as the lounge, gift shop, dayroom, or, if the weather permits, the outdoor lounges. If the resident can take trips away, use the visiting time to go to a restaurant, shopping center, religious service, cultural event, or for a drive. If the resident's condition permits, an occasional visit home or to a friend or relative can contribute to maintaining relationships and a link to life. When possible, include the resident's roommate and other nursing home acquaintances in some part of the visit. This involvement can help the resident adjust.

Conversing and Visiting

The resident needs to be part of a normal conversation and encouraged both to talk and to listen. Unpleasant news should be discussed along with good news. Keeping bad news away from elders, when they are alert, can make them feel left out, and if they find out from someone else, it can breed distrust. When appropriate, ask for advice or an opinion; this gives the resident reassurance that he or she is still considered a part of the family.

Some caregivers avoid visits because they are afraid of being asked difficult questions. A good guideline is to tell the truth in a gentle, firm, calm, and straightforward manner and not to become involved in a no-win discussion. For example, the caregiver can feel guilty if the resident repeatedly asks, "When can I go home?", or "Why can't I go back home to your house?" The caregiver should answer, "I wish we could take you back to your home or my home, but you need 24-hour, professional care, and I cannot give you that kind of care or I can't arrange for that kind of care in your home." The caregiver should add that the nursing home is the resident's home. If the resident may be able to leave after a period of recovery, this can be part of the caregiver's response. The answers have to fit the mental awareness and the reality of the situation. Some questions may have to be answered over and over again till the resident and family members and friends have come to accept the nursing home.

Special Listening

Listening well involves trying to hear what is felt as well as what is being said, what is meant as well as what the words are. The statement, "I am always alone in this place," may mean, "I do not feel anything for the people here nor they for me."

The resident may be asking for more positive interaction at the nursing home or for more tangible signs of interest and affection from the staff such as being touched on the shoulder or hand, or being called by the first name. A smile or an acknowledgment by small gestures conveys, I like you, you are nice, you mean something, you are a person.

If the resident complains that things are being stolen from the room, the caregiver should first determine whether the items are missing or not. If something has been misplaced, the resident may be feeling that independence has been taken away. The accusations of theft are not for tangible objects but for the intangible ones of independence, privacy, and uniqueness. The caregiver can discuss these feelings with the resident.

Sensory Stimulation

A person confined in a nursing home experiences some degree of sensory deprivation, which can be heightened by the sensory impairments that many older people have. An effective caregiver can provide stimulation and help the individual enjoy the world through the five senses by bringing colorful items to see, food and snacks to taste, soft objects to feel, and music or spoken words to listen to. Sensory losses accelerate as people age. The visiting caregiver should observe changes and report them to the appropriate staff member.

Together the caregiver and staff can make an effort to compensate for a resident's deteriorating vision by using large-print material, arranging for an eye examination, and having eyeglasses checked and changed if needed. If the person is having difficulty hearing, compensating techniques for communication should be used by the staff and the family. If the elderly person seems to be uninterested in food, provide special food and beverages. Always check first to find out if such food items are allowed with the person's medication or special diet. Check that dentures fit properly and that there is no gum problem.

Sensory experiences are more meaningful and intense when shared with the caregiver and others important to the elderly person. Visiting time is the logical time, while the resident and the visitor are interacting and their relationship is being reinforced. The nursing home's social workers, activities director, and volunteer coordinator may be able to help with ideas and activities for sensory experiences.

The Caregiver as an Ombudsman

During visits the caregiver may hear a lot of complaints from the nursing home resident. These are to be expected, since being in one place with life organized in a routine can make a person testy. The caregiver is probably the only person the elderly person feels will listen and help. Complaints may be ways of saying, "I don't like being here," or "I am not getting any attention," or "I have no say over anything." They may also be ways of letting the caregiver know that more attention is needed.

Some complaints may be exaggerations, and some may arise because the resident does not understand that the staff has routines and that attention and help will be available in accordance with schedules. The caregiver needs to evaluate all the complaints. Legitimate complaints should be brought to the attention of the correct staff person. Complaints and problems should be taken seriously by the caregiver and discussed with the staff with understanding. Staff members should also be complimented for the care and concern they show.

It is important for the caregiver to take part in regularly scheduled care conferences or resident's progress meetings. These conferences or meetings usually involve the social worker, head nurse, activities director, nutritionist, and other staff personnel. This is the time to go over schedules, discuss any current complaints or issues raised by the resident, and assess the progress of the resident's adjustment. The staff may have some suggestions for the caregiver's activities with the resident and for changes in diet, social activities, and medical attention. The aides who spend a great deal of time with the resident can give the caregiver another point of view and should be asked for comments. The caregiver should speak to the aides on more than one shift. If the nursing home has a family night, family members or friends should attend and use the meetings as a time to communicate with the nursing home staff.

Some caregivers discover that their continual involvement with the nursing home resident is emotionally stressful or even a reliving of the trauma of the initial decision to place the resident in the nursing home. Some homes have a caregiver support group to help with these feelings. Caregivers can also look for support groups in the community or one-to-one therapy. Caregivers and others involved with the elderly person need to understand that nursing home placement is not abandonment but an act of love and concern. They should not view the nursing home placement as a sign of failure but as a realistic response to the needs of the elderly person and the caregiver's abilities and limits.

When the need for a nursing home occurs, caregivers may be weighed down with guilt and disappointment. These feelings are compounded by the pressures of the family, friends, and neighbors and by larger societal pressures and implied expectations. Living in a nursing home cannot take the place of living at home in reasonably good health until death comes. But that choice is not always possible.

Some elderly people never need the care that a nursing home offers, but for those who do, families can be grateful that nursing homes exist. These facilities can be positively viewed as a home where elderly people live within the limits of their age and physical and mental conditions. Then caregivers can shift from the role of giving hands-on care to the role of a concerned, active nursing home visitor and ombudsman.

References

American Association of Retired Persons (AARP). *The Right Place at the Right Time: A Guide to Long-Term Care Choices.* Washington, DC: AARP, 1987.

Bonjean, Marilyn J. *Making Visits Count: A Guidebook for Nursing Home Visitors.* Madison: Wisconsin Vocational Studies Center, University of Wisconsin-Madison, n.d.

Forrest, Mary Brumpey, et al. *Nursing Homes: The Complete Guide*. New York: Facts on File, 1990.

Karr, Katherine L. *Promises To Keep: The Family's Role in Nursing Home Care.* New York: Prometheus Books, 1991.

AARP. Health Advocacy Services Program Department. *Nursing Home Life: A Guide for Residents and Families.* Washington, DC: AARP, 1987.

Pieper, Hanns G. *The Nursing Home Primer: A Comprehensive Guide to Nursing Homes and Other Long-Term Care Options.* White Hall, VA: Betterway Publications, 1989.

Vierck, Elizabeth. *Paying for Health Care after Age 65.* Santa Barbara, CA: ABC-CLIO, 1990.

Resources

Chapter 8

Resource Organizations

Aging and Health Professionals Organizations

American Association of Homes for the Aging (AAHA)
Sheldon Goldberg, President
901 E Street, NW, Suite 500
Washington, DC 20004
(202) 783-2242

> AAHA is a membership organization of not-for-profit housing providers for the elderly. AAHA promotes the interest of its members through education to enhance their ability to serve their constituents. Consumers can order a series of five consumer brochures on housing options for the elderly for $1. State associations can be contacted through the national office.

American Health Care Association (AHCA)
Paul R. Willging, Executive Vice President
1201 L Street, NW
Washington, DC 20005
(202) 842-4444
(800) 321-0343 (publications only)

> AHCA is a trade association representing the nursing home industry. AHCA offers professional development training programs and resource materials for long-term care administrators, nurses, and nurse aides. The organization distributes free consumer brochures on selecting, paying for, and visiting nursing homes. State affiliates can be contacted through the national office.

Center on Rural Elderly
James Galliher, Director
University of Missouri-Kansas City
5245 Rockhill Road
Kansas City, MO 64110
(816) 235-2180

> The Center on Rural Elderly provides educational resources, materials, information, technical assistance, and referrals to practitioners in rural and urban areas. The center's target issues are health education and promotion, caregiver training, intergenerational programming, leadership training, and minority programming. It provides information, referral, and self-help materials to family caregivers. For $12, the center offers the *Directory of Education Programs for Caregivers of Elders* containing 72 program profiles. The center also distributes *Reducing Barriers to Participation in Family Caregiver Training* for $8.

Continuing Care Accredation Commission (CCAC)
Ann Gillespie, Director
1129 20th Street, NW, Suite 400
Washington, DC 20036
(202) 828-9439

> CCAC is an accrediting organization for continuing care communities. Accredited facilities must meet CCAC standards. CCAC offers a free listing of accredited communities.

ElderMed America
Roberta Suber, Executive Vice President
20500 Nordhoff Street
Chatsworth, CA 91311
(818) 407-2221
(800) 227-3463

> ElderMed America helps hospitals implement membership services for older adults. ElderMed memberships are free to older adults and include information and referral, health education and screening, discounts, and caregiver education and support. Services vary by hospital site.

Families USA Foundation
Ron Pollack, Executive Director

1334 G Street, NW
Washington, DC 20005
(202) 628-3030

> The Families USA Foundation is a nonprofit organization dedi-
> cated to preserving and strengthening the security and dignity of
> older Americans and their families. The foundation provides
> public policy information to advocates and activists on senior
> health, long-term care, and income security issues. *A.S.A.P.*, a
> federal legislative alert, is available free of charge to advocates
> who agree to actively lobby on the issues.

Foundation for Hospice and Homecare
William Halamandaris, Chief Executive Officer
519 C Street, NE
Washington, DC 20002
(202) 547-6586

> The foundation seeks to improve the quality of life for American
> citizens with an emphasis on the needs of the dying, disabled, dis-
> advantaged, and elderly. The foundation provides homemaker
> and home-health agencies with certification curriculum. Consum-
> ers can order a free publication on how to choose a hospice or
> home-care agency by sending a self-addressed business envelope.

Health Insurance Association of America (HIAA)
Carl Schramm, President
1025 Connecticut Avenue, NW, Suite 1200
Washington, DC 20036
(202) 223-7780

> HIAA is a membership organization of insurance companies. The
> association provides two free publications to consumers on how
> to evaluate long-term care and Medicare supplemental insurance
> policies. Publications can be ordered from HIAA, P.O. Box
> 41455, Washington, DC 20018. The association does not recom-
> mend specific insurance companies or policies.

National Academy of Elder Law Attorneys
Laury Adsit, Staff Director
655 North Alvernon Way, Suite 108
Tucson, AZ 85711
(602) 881-4005

The academy helps its members provide quality legal services to the elderly. It offers numerous training programs for attorneys specializing in elder law and a free consumer publication on *How To Choose an Elder Law Attorney*. The academy does not make referrals to individual attorneys.

National Aging Resource Center on Elder Abuse (NARCEA)
Toshio Tatara, Director
c/o American Public Welfare Association
810 First Street, NE, Suite 500
Washington, DC 20002
(202) 682-2470

NARCEA works primarily with state adult protective services departments to conduct research and provide public education on elder abuse. The center offers a number of publications for professionals including an analysis of state elder abuse legislation, highlights of a national teleconference, and guidelines for gathering and reporting elder abuse. The center also distributes the *Elder Abuse Video Resources Guide* for $7 and *Elder Abuse: An Information Guide for Professionals and Concerned Citizen*, which costs $3 per copy for 100 copies, $2.50 per copy for 100–200 copies, and $2 per copy for 200 copies or more (100 copy minimum order).

National Association for Home Care (NAHC)
Val J. Halamandaris, President
519 C Street, NE
Stanton Park
Washington, DC 20002
(202) 547-7424

NAHC is a trade association representing the interests of home-care agencies. The association sponsors research, promotes home and hospice care, lobbies, and provides expert advice to members. It offers home-care providers numerous training and educational materials. NAHC does not provide services to family caregivers.

National Association of Social Workers (NASW)
Mark G. Battle, Executive Director

7981 Eastern Avenue
Silver Spring, MD 20910
(301) 565-0333
(800) 638-8799

> NASW is an organization of professional social workers that develops practice standards, works for responsible public social policy, and raises public awareness of pressing social issues. NASW offers printed materials and workshops on caregiving for professionals at state and national conferences. NASW distributes *The Family Caregiving Crisis,* an overview of the issue, for $8.95.

National Association of State Units on Aging (NASUA)
Daniel A. Quirk, Executive Director
2033 K Street, NW, Suite 304
Washington, DC 20006
(202) 785-0707

> NASUA, a membership association of state departments on aging, seeks to improve the services of its members by monitoring legislation and providing training and technical assistance. Professionals can use resources through the Center for the Advancement of State Community Care Programs, the Information and Referral Support Center, and the National Center for State Long-Term Care Ombudsman Resources. Each state department on aging is listed in the Regional and State Resources sections of this chapter.

National Citizens' Coalition for Nursing Home Reform (NCCNHR)
Elma Holder, Executive Director
1224 M Street, NW, Suite 301
Washington, DC 20005
(202) 393-2018

> NCCNHR is a consumer-based, nonprofit membership organization of local and state groups and individuals dedicated to improving health care and quality of life for nursing home residents. It provides information, training, consultation, regulatory monitoring, and advocacy. NCCNHR issues a newsletter, the *Quality Care Advocate,* and a number of other publications geared toward the professional.

National Council on the Aging (NCOA)
Dr. Daniel Thursz, President
409 Third Street, SW
Washington, DC 20024
(202) 479-1200

> NCOA is a national, nonprofit membership organization work-
> ing to make society more responsive to older people and serving
> as a resource for program development, training, research, infor-
> mation and referral, and advocacy. The organization provides
> professionals with workshops and manuals on respite, adult day
> care, and caregiving in the workplace. NCOA also distributes
> resource materials to family members such as *Caregiving Tips*
> for $4 and the *Family Home Caring Guides* for $5.

National Hospice Association
John J. Mahoney, President
1901 Moore Street, Suite 901
Arlington, VA 22209
(800) 658-8898 (referrals and general information only)
(703) 243-5900

> The association is a membership organization of hospice pro-
> gram providers that seeks to promote the concept of hospice,
> foster better health care practice in hospices, and advance the
> rights of the terminally ill. The organization offers the public a
> free basic information packet. It also offers four seminars per
> year for professional hospice providers.

National Interfaith Coalition on Aging (NICA)
Rev. John Evans, Manager
c/o NCOA
409 Third Street, SW, Second Floor
Washington, DC 20024
(202) 479-6689
(800) 424-9046

> NICA, part of the National Council on the Aging, seeks to enable
> religious organizations to serve older adults. NICA provides
> training and resource materials to congregations interested in
> caregiving issues.

Caregiver Services and Resource Organizations

Action
Jane A. Kenny, Director
Older American Volunteer Program
1100 Vermont Avenue, NW
Washington, DC 20525
(202) 606-5135

> The Older American Volunteer Program of Action provides volunteer opportunities for more than 450,000 senior citizens. The agency operates the Senior Companion Program, in which seniors offer companionship to isolated seniors, and the Retired Senior Volunteer Program, which offers seniors meaningful volunteer opportunities within 1,200 local projects throughout the United States.

Aging Network Services, Inc.
Barbara Kane and Grace Lebow, Cofounders
Topaz House
4400 East West Highway
Bethesda, MD 20814
(301) 657-4329
(800) 477-4267

> Aging Network Services is a national network of 250 private geriatric social workers who offer counseling, support groups, information and referral, and care management services to older people and their caregivers. The organization also offers care management services for employers.

Alzheimer's Association
Edward Truschke, President
919 North Michigan Avenue, Suite 1000
Chicago, IL 60611
(312) 853-3060
(800) 272-3900 (patients and families only)

> The Alzheimer's Association is dedicated to raising public awareness, lobbying for federal support, and assisting family members of Alzheimer's disease patients. The association produces

numerous resource materials on research updates, diagnosis, patient care, and social services. Contact the national office to locate chapters throughout the United States.

American Diabetes Association (ADA)
John H. Graham, Chief Executive Officer
National Center
1660 Duke Street
Alexandria, VA 22314
(703) 549-1500
(800) 232-3472

> ADA is a voluntary health organization concerned with diabetes and its complications. Through its state affiliate associations, ADA offers classes and support groups for consumers and educational programs for health care professionals. Moderately priced ADA consumer brochures cover issues such as a general overview of diabetes, nutrition, and children and diabetes. The association offers a number of professional journals containing the latest medical and scientific information. *The Physician's Guide to Non-Insulin Dependent Diabetes* provides information on treatment and complications. The cost of this book is $19.95 plus $4.50 for shipping and handling.

American Parkinson Disease Association (APDA)
Frank L. Williams, Executive Director
60 Bay Street, Suite 401
Staten Island, NY 10301
(718) 981-8001
(800) 223-2732
West Coast office
13743 Victory Boulevard
Van Nuys, CA 91401
(818) 908-9951

> APDA is a nonprofit organization funding research and providing information and referral, public education, and counseling on Parkinson's disease. The organization offers information and referral at 43 centers throughout the country and maintains 80 local chapters. All services are free.

Catholic Charities USA
Rev. Thomas J. Harvey, Executive Director
1731 King Street, Suite 200
Alexandria, VA 22314
(703) 549-1390

> Catholic Charities USA is a nationwide network of more than 800 agencies, institutions, and individuals who aim to reduce poverty, support families, and assist communities. Services offered by members include respite, chore services, caregiver retreats, friendly visitors, adult day care, counseling, and meals-on-wheels.

Children of Aging Parents (CAPS)
Woodbourne Office Campus
1609 Woodbourne Road, Suite 302A
Levittown, PA 19057
(215) 945-6900

> CAPS is a nonprofit membership organization dedicated to the needs of caregivers of the elderly. The organization is developing a national network of support groups and offers information and referral services and a newsletter, *The Capsule*. CAPS also distributes low-cost leaflets on a variety of topics.

Continence Restored, Inc.
E. Douglas Whitehear and Anne Smith-Young, Directors
785 Park Avenue
New York, NY 10021
(212) 879-3131

> Continence Restored disseminates information on bladder control problems. The organization sponsors a nationwide network of support groups and offers information and referrals to consumers and professionals.

Elder Care Solutions
Merrily Orsini, President
1220 Bardstown Road
Louisville, KY 40204
(502) 452-9644
(800) 633-5723

Elder Care Solutions provides quality in-home care and care management in partnership with families in the least restrictive setting for older adults. The company distributes *How To Care for the Elderly in Their Own Homes,* a series of 11 30-minute audiotapes on caregiving techniques, for $99.

Huntington's Disease Society of America (HDSA)
Stephen Bajardi, Executive Director
140 West 22nd Street, Sixth Floor
New York, NY 10011
(212) 242-1968
(800) 345-4372 (for families and patients only)

HDSA is dedicated to finding a cure for Huntington's disease and improving the lives of patients and their caregivers. HDSA offers information and referral services, moderately priced educational materials, and videotapes. The national office of HDSA makes referrals to the 32 local chapters around the country.

Medic Alert Foundation International
Kenneth W. Harms, President
2323 Colorado Avenue
Turlock, CA 95380
(209) 669-2402
(800) 344-3226

The Medic Alert Foundation provides methods of recording and communicating personal medical information to protect and save lives. The foundation offers personal emergency response systems and medical alert bracelets and neck chains.

National Association of Private Geriatric Care Managers (NAPGCM)
Laury Adsit, Executive Director
655 North Alvernon Way, Suite 108
Tucson, AZ 86711
(602) 882-4005

NAPGCM is an association of private practitioners who provide care management services for the elderly. Some members also offer money management, home-care, psychotherapy, and medical claims filing services. The association refers caregivers and seniors to case managers operating in their locations.

National Association of Area Agencies on Aging (N4A)
Jon Linkous, Director
1112 16th Street, NW, Suite 100
Washington, DC 20036
(202) 296-8130
(800) 677-1116 (Eldercare Locator Service)

> N4A is a membership organization for the 670 Area Agencies on Aging across the country. The nationwide Eldercare Locator Service helps caregivers identify community services for the elderly. Callers should present the name, address, and ZIP code of the older person who needs care.

National Consumers League
Linda Golodner, Executive Director
815 15th Street, NW, Suite 928-N
Washington, DC 20005
(202) 639-8140

> This is a private membership group that conducts research, education, and advocacy for workers and consumers. The organization produces a series of consumer guides to health care including guides to hospice care, home-health care, and life-care communities, priced at $2 each for members and $4 for nonmembers.

National Federation of Interfaith Volunteer Caregivers
Virginia Schiaffino, Executive Director
105 Mary's Avenue
P.O. Box 1939
Kingston, NY 12401
(914) 331-1358

> The federation seeks to strengthen and expand the ministry of caregiving throughout the United States. The organization offers information and referral to local interfaith projects that provide direct services to family caregivers. It also provides technical assistance to others interested in developing or enhancing a caregivers program. *The Handbook for Interfaith Volunteer Caregiving,* a manual outlining program development steps, is available for $25.

National Stroke Association
Thelma Edwards, Director of Program Development

300 East Hampden Avenue, Suite 240
Englewood, CO 80110
(303) 762-9922
(800) 787-6537

> The National Stroke Association seeks to reduce the frequency, severity, and impact of strokes. The organization publishes a number of brochures to help family members cope with stroke patients.

The Simon Foundation
Cheryle Gartley, President
P.O. Box 815
Wilmette, IL 60091
(708) 864-3913
(800) 237-4666 (patient information)

> The Simon Foundation seeks to increase public awareness of incontinence, remove the social stigma attached to this disability, and provide patient education. The foundation offers a series of seven videos for health professionals on understanding and treating incontinence. It also distributes a quarterly newsletter, *The Informer,* and the book, *Managing Incontinence: A Guide to Living with the Loss of Bladder Control,* for $12.95.

United Parkinson Foundation
Oudy Rosner, Executive Director
360 West Superior Street
Chicago, IL 60610
(312) 664-2344

> The United Parkinson Foundation is an international membership organization dedicated to patient education and support of research on Parkinson's disease. The foundation distributes background information, exercise materials, and newsletters. The foundation also offers educational symposia for patients and families and awards research grants.

United Seniors Health Cooperative
James P. Firman, Director
1331 H Street, NW, Suite 500
Washington, DC 20005
(202) 393-6222

United Seniors Health Cooperative is a membership organization for seniors that seeks to help older people achieve health, independence, and financial security. The cooperative offers health and long-term care insurance counseling for members along with consumer publications on choosing a nursing home and paying for long-term care. For $10 each, it offers *Long-Term Care Insurance: A Professional Guide to Selecting Policies* and *Managing Your Health Care Finances,* a guide explaining Medicare and Medigap insurance.

Visiting Nurse Associations of America (VNAA)
Laurie Eugenbanks, Acting Chief Executive Officer
3801 East Florida Avenue, Suite 206
Denver, CO 80210
(303) 753-0218
(800) 426-2547 (referral line)

VNAA is committed to unifying visiting nurse organizations and strengthening the position of VNAA affiliates in the home-care marketplace. The toll-free telephone number can be used by both family members and professionals to locate any Visiting Nurse Association in the United States.

Volunteers of America, Inc.
J. Clint Cheveallier, President
3813 North Causeway Boulevard
Metairie, LA 70002
(504) 837-2652

Volunteers of America is a movement organized to reach and uplift all people. Through local affiliates, the organization offers a number of services for the elderly including homemakers, home-delivered meals, housing, information and referral, and senior citizen centers. Specific local services vary.

General Aging Organizations

American Association of Retired Persons (AARP)
Horace B. Deets, Executive Director
601 E Street, NW
Washington, DC 20049
(202) 434-2277

AARP is a nonprofit membership organization dedicated to addressing the needs of people age 50 and older. The association offers a home-care skills-building course for family members, called Home Is Where the Care Is, and a number of free publications for caregivers. Several publications are available in Spanish. AARP also distributes *Caregivers in the Workplace* for $15, a series of how-to booklets to help employers support employees who are caregivers. AARP's regional offices are listed in the Regional and State Resources sections of this chapter.

Administration on Aging (AoA)

Joyce Berry, U.S. Commissioner on Aging
330 Independence Avenue, SW
Washington, DC 20201
(202) 619-0641

The AoA, located in the U.S. Department of Health and Human Services, is the federal agency devoted exclusively to the concerns of America's older population. AoA funds and supports the National Network on Aging, which is comprised of 57 state and 670 area agencies on aging. The AoA regional offices are listed in the Regional Resources section of this chapter.

National Institute on Aging (NIA)

Gene D. Cohen, Acting Director
9000 Rockville Pike
Bethesda, MD 20892
(301) 496-4000

The NIA, part of the National Institutes of Health, is the federal government's principal agency for conducting and supporting biomedical, social, and behavioral research related to the aging process and the diseases of older people. NIA distributes a number of free resource materials including a series of *Age Pages,* fact sheets that provide information about how people age, disorders and diseases of older people, health promotion, safety, medical care, and nutrition.

Self-Help Organizations

American Self-Help Clearinghouse

Edward Madara, Executive Director

St Clares-Riverside Medical Center
25 Pocono Road
Denville, NJ 07834
(201) 625-7101

> The clearinghouse provides current information and contacts for national self-help groups, maintains information on model programs, and offers technical assistance for establishing self-help groups. The clearinghouse publishes the *Self-Help Sourcebook*, a listing of over 600 national and model groups.

National Self-Help Clearinghouse
Frank Riessman, Director
25 West 43rd Street, Room 620
New York, NY 10036
(212) 642-2944

> The National Self-Help Clearinghouse facilitates access to self-help groups around the country and works to increase awareness of the importance of mutual support. The clearinghouse offers referrals to support groups. *The Self-Help Reporter,* a quarterly newsletter, is available for $10 and the booklet, *How To Organize a Self-Help Group,* is available for $6.

Work Site Caregiving Resources

Aging Resource Management Services, Inc. (ARMS)
Jacqueline Sarantis, Director
2975 Independence Avenue
Bronx, NY 10463
(212) 543-3671

> ARMS provides caregiving services to corporations, insurance companies, and employee assistance programs. Services include management awareness seminars, national information and referral, employee caregiver educational seminars, and support groups. The newsletter, *Eldercare Memo,* is available to the general public.

Dependent Care Connection (DCC)
John Bassett Place, President

P.O. Box 2783
Westport, CT 06880
(203) 226-2680

> DCC provides companies with counseling and referral services for child and elderly care. Employees at client companies can call a toll-free telephone number to discuss options for fulfilling dependent-care needs. DCC maintains a database of child and elderly care providers across the country and refers employees to services within their locations. DCC also provides videos and printed resource materials to clients.

Elder Care Insights (ECI)
Elisabeth A. Bryenton, President
19111 Detroit Road, Suite 104
Rocky River, OH 44116
(216) 356-2900

> Elder Care Insights, a subsidiary of Child Care Insights, provides consulting services to employers interested in implementing elder care programs. ECI also works with individuals and families in search of elder care options. The company operates Elderbase, a comprehensive, national database of services for the elderly.

Families and Work Institute
Dana Friedman, President
330 Seventh Avenue
New York, NY 10001
(202) 465-2044

> The institute works with businesses, government agencies, and community groups to help people balance the demands of work and family. The organization conducts research on corporate work and family policies and demographics. The Families and Work Institute offers individual consultation and management training with companies.

Partnership for Eldercare
Barbara B. Lepis, Director
280 Broadway, Room 214
New York, NY 10007
(212) 577-8631

The partnership is a program that helps employers support working caregivers with referral services, seminars, support groups, and benefits information booths. The organization provides technical assistance to aging organizations interested in developing corporate caregiving programs. *Establishing a Partnership for Eldercare,* a technical guide, is available for $10.

The Partnership Group, Inc.
Tyler Phillips, President
840 West Main Street
Lansdale, PA 19446
(215) 362-5070

The Partnership Group provides employers with resource and referral services, consultation, and workshops for employee caregivers. It also provides managerial training on caregiving. The company does not offer services to the general public.

Washington Business Group on Health (WBGH)
Mary Jane England, President
Institute on Aging, Work, and Health
777 North Capital Street, Suite 800
Washington, DC 20003
(202) 408-9320

WBGH represents member companies on health-care policy issues. The institute publishes two guides for employers interested in employee caregiver issues. *An Employer's Guide to Eldercare,* a guidebook written to help human resources professionals become more knowledgeable about caregiving issues in the workplace, can be purchased for $18. *Public/Private Partnerships in Aging,* a booklet providing information to the aging network on how to work with businesses on caregiving issues, is available for $8.

Work and Family Clearinghouse
Elsie Vartanian, Women's Bureau Director
Women's Bureau
U.S. Department of Labor
200 Constitution Avenue, NW, Room S3317
Washington, DC 20210
(800) 827-5335

The Work and Family Clearinghouse encourages employers to implement quality dependent-care programs and policies. The clearinghouse provides employers with implementation guides for various dependent-care programs, profiles of model programs and policies, and has a referral network of nonprofit resource organizations. The clearinghouse does not respond to consumer requests.

Regional Resources

Administration on Aging (AoA) Regional Offices

AoA Region 1 Office
John F. Kennedy Building, Room 501
Boston, MA 02203
(617) 565-1158

AoA Region 2 Office
26 Federal Plaza, Room 4149
Broadway and Worth Streets
New York, NY 10278
(212) 264-2976

AoA Region 3 Office
3535 Market Street
P.O. Box 13716
Philadelphia, PA 19101
(215) 596-6891

AoA Region 4 Office
101 Marietta Tower, Suite 903
Atlanta, GA 30323
(404) 331-5900

AoA Region 5 Office
105 West Adams Street, 21st Floor
Chicago, IL 60603
(312) 353-3141

AoA Region 6 Office
1200 Main Tower Building, Room 1000
Dallas, TX 75202
(214) 767-2971

AoA Region 7 Office
601 East 12th Street, Room 384
Kansas City, MO 64106
(816) 426-2955

AoA Region 8 Office
1961 Stout Street, Room 1185
Federal Office Building
Denver, CO 80294
(303) 844-2951

AoA Region 9 Office
50 United Nations Plaza, Room 480
San Francisco, CA 94102
(415) 556-6003

AoA Region 10 Office
Blanchard Plaza, RX-33, Room 600
2201 Sixth Avenue
Seattle, WA 98121
(206) 553-5341

American Association of Retired Persons (AARP) Regional Offices

AARP Area 1 Office
Park Square Building
31 Saint James Avenue
Boston, MA 02116
(617) 426-1185

AARP Area 2 Office
919 Third Avenue, 9th Floor
New York, NY 10022
(212) 758-1411

AARP Area 3 Office
1600 Duke Street, 2nd Floor
Alexandria, VA 22314
(703) 739-9220

AARP Area 4 Office
999 Peachtree Street, NE
Atlanta, GA 30309
(404) 888-0077

AARP Area 5 Office
2720 Des Plaines Avenue, Suite 113
Des Plaines, IL 60018
(708) 298-2852

AARP Area 6 Office
1901 West 47th Place, Suite 104
Westwood, KS 66205
(923) 831-6000

AARP Area 7 Office
8144 Walnut Hill Lane, Suite 700, LB-39
Dallas, TX 75231
(214) 361-3060

AARP Area 8 Office
709 Kearns Building
136 South Main Street
Salt Lake City, UT 84101
(801) 328-0691

AARP Area 9 Office
4201 Long Beach Boulevard, Suite 422
Long Beach, CA 90807
(213) 427-9611

AARP Area 10 Office
9750 Third Avenue, NE, Suite 400
Seattle, WA 98115
(206) 526-7918

State Resources

Brookdale Center on Aging of Hunter College
Adele Goldberg, Director
425 East 25th Street
New York, NY 10010
(212) 481-7670

> The Brookdale Center on Aging is a gerontological institute affiliated with Hunter College. The center offers a community-based respite program for dementia patients, support groups, and information and referral. The center distributes a 55-minute video on caregiving hosted by Hugh Downs, *In Care Of: Families and Their Elders*. The video rents for $50 and sells for $295 for VHS and $345 for U-Matic.

Coalition of Advocates for the Rights of the Infirm Elderly (CARIE)
Bernice Soffer, Executive Director
1315 Walnut Street, Suite 1000
Philadelphia, PA 19107
(215) 545-5728

> CARIE works to ensure that older people's rights are protected. CARIE Line is a free telephone consultation service that handles

complaints, resolves problems, provides information and referral, and offers special assistance to victims of elder abuse. CARIE also offers the Caregiver Assistance Service to employers. The Caregiver Coalition is a statewide group supporting caregivers of adults by consolidating the knowledge and experience of its members and providing technical assistance to other organizations.

Duke Family Support Program
Lisa Gwyther, Director
P.O. Box 3600
Duke Medical Center
Durham, NC 27710
(919) 684-2328
(800) 672-4213 (North Carolina residents only)

> The Duke Family Support Program is an information and referral resource for family caregivers of people with memory loss. The program offers support group meetings, a toll-free hotline, written resource materials, and a quarterly newsletter, *The Caregiver*. The program offers seminars, training, and educational videocassettes for professionals.

Family Survival Project
Kathleen A. Kelly, Executive Director
425 Bush Street, Suite 500
San Francisco, CA 94108
(415) 434-3388
(800) 445-8106 (California only)

> The project is a statewide organization seeking to improve the emotional, physical, and financial situations of brain-impaired adults and their families. It also increases recognition of the consequences of brain disorders by policymakers and the general public. The organization offers information and referral, consultation, subsidized respite care, education, training, and support groups for family members, as well as training, technical assistance, and research for professionals. It publishes a number of moderately priced reports, research studies, fact sheets, training materials, the *Directory of California Support Groups,* and the annual volume of *Clearinghouse Collections,* containing nearly 900 annotations of publications.

Vision Foundation, Inc.
Barbara R. Kibler, Director
818 Mt. Auburn Street
Watertown, MA 02172
(617) 926-4232
(800) 852-3029 (Massachusetts only)

> The foundation provides self-help services to individuals coping with sight loss, their families, and the professionals who serve them. The foundation provides consumers and professionals with information and referral, training, educational seminars, large-print informational materials, and audiocassette tapes.

State Departments on Aging

Alabama
Alabama Commission on Aging
136 Catoma Street, 2nd Floor
Montgomery, AL 36130
(205) 242-5743

Alaska
Older Alaskans Commission
P.O. Box C, MS 0209
Juneau, AL 99811
(907) 465-3250

Arizona
Aging and Adult Administration
Department of Economic Security
1400 West Washington Street
Phoenix, AZ 85007
(800) 352-3792 (Arizona only)
(602) 542-4446

Arkansas
Division of Aging and Adult Services
Arkansas Department of Human
    Service
Main and 7th Streets
Donaghey Building, Suite 1428
Little Rock, AR 72201
(501) 682-2441

California
California Department of Aging
1600 K Street
Sacramento, CA 95814
(916) 322-5290

Colorado
Aging and Adult Services
Department of Social Services
1575 Sherman Street, 10th Floor
Denver, CO 80203
(303) 866-5905

Connecticut
Connecticut Department on Aging
175 Main Street
Hartford, CT 06106
(800) 443-9946 (Connecticut only)
(203) 566-3238

Delaware
Delaware Division on Aging
Department of Health and Social
    Services
1901 North Dupont Highway,
    2nd Floor
New Castle, DE 19720
(800) 223-9074 (Delaware only)
(302) 421-6791

District of Columbia
District of Columbia Office on Aging
Executive Office of the Mayor
1424 K Street, NW, 2nd Floor
Washington, DC 20005
(202) 724-5622

Florida
Aging and Adult Services
Department of Health and
  Rehabilitative Services
Building 2, Room 328
1323 Winewood Boulevard
Tallahassee, FL 32399
(800) 342-0825 (Florida only)
(904) 488-8922

Georgia
Department of Human Resources
878 Peachtree Street, NE, 6th Floor
Atlanta, GA 30309
(404) 894-5333

Hawaii
Hawaii Executive Office on Aging
335 Merchant Street, Room 241
Honolulu, HI 96813
(808) 548-2593

Idaho
Idaho Office on Aging
Statehouse, Room 108
Boise, ID 83720
(208) 334-3833

Illinois
Illinois Department on Aging
421 East Capitol Avenue
Springfield, IL 62701
(800) 252-8966 (Illinois only)
(217) 785-2870

Indiana
Indiana Department of Human Services
251 North Illinois Street
P.O. Box 7083
Indianapolis, IN 46207
(800) 545-7763 (Indiana only)
(317) 232-1139

Iowa
Department of Elder Affairs
Jewett Building, Suite 236
914 Grand Avenue
Des Moines, IA 50319
(800) 532-3213 (Iowa only)
(515) 281-5187

Kansas
Kansas Department on Aging
Docking State Office Building, 122-S
915 Southwest Harrison
Topeka, KS 66612
(800) 432-3535 (Kansas only)
(913) 296-4986

Kentucky
Division for Aging Services
Cabinet for Human Resources
Department for Social Services
275 East Main Street
Frankfort, KY 40621
(501) 564-6930

Louisiana
Governor's Office of Elderly Affairs
P.O. Box 80374
Baton Rouge, LA 70898
(504) 925-1700

Maine
Bureau of Maine's Elderly
Department of Human Services
State House Station 11
Augusta, ME 04333
(207) 626-5335

Maryland
Maryland Office on Aging
301 West Preston Street
Baltimore, MD 21201
(800) 338-0153 (Maryland only)
(301) 225-1102

Massachusetts
Massachusetts Executive Office of Elder
  Affairs
38 Chauncy Street
Boston, MA 02111
(800) 882-2003 (Massachusetts only)
(617) 727-7750

Michigan
Office of Services to the Aging
P.O. Box 30026
Lansing, MI 48909
(517) 373-8230

Minnesota
Minnesota Board on Aging
444 Lafayette Road, 4th Floor
St. Paul, MN 55155
(800) 652-9747 (Minnesota only)
(612) 296-2770

Mississippi
Council on Aging
Division of Aging and Adult Services
421 West Pascagoula Street
Jackson, MS 39203
(800) 222-7622 (Mississippi only)
(601) 949-2070

Missouri
Division of Aging
Department of Social Services
2701 West Main Street
P.O. Box 1337
Jefferson City, MO 65102
(800) 235-5503 (Missouri only)
(314) 751-3082

Montana
Governor's Office of Aging
Capitol Station, Room 219
Helena, MT 59620
(800) 332-2272
(406) 444-3111

Nebraska
Department on Aging
301 Centennial Mall South
P.O. Box 95044
Lincoln, NE 68509
(402) 471-2306

Nevada
Division for Aging Services
State Mail Room
Las Vegas, NV 89158
(702) 486-3545

New Hampshire
Division of Elderly and Adult Services
New Hampshire Department of Health
  and Human Services
6 Hazen Drive
Concord, NH 03301
(800) 852-3311 (New Hampshire only)
(603) 271-4390

New Jersey
New Jersey Division on Aging
Department of Community Affairs
101 South Broad Street, CN 807
Trenton, NJ 08625
(800) 792-8820 (New Jersey only)
(609) 292-0920

New Mexico
New Mexico State Agency on Aging
La Villa Rivera Building, 4th Floor
224 East Palace Avenue
Santa Fe, NM 87501
(800) 432-2080 (New Mexico only)
(505) 827-7640

New York
New York State Office for the Aging
Agency Building 2, Empire State Plaza
Albany, NY 12223
(800) 342-9871
(518) 474-5731

North Carolina
North Carolina Division of Aging
Department of Human Resources
Kirby Building
1985 Umstead Drive
Raleigh, NC 27603
(800) 662-7030
(919) 733-3983

North Dakota
Aging Services Division
North Dakota Department of Human
  Services
State Capitol Building
Bismarck, ND 58505
(800) 472-2622
(701) 224-2577

Ohio
Ohio Department of Aging
50 West Broad Street, 9th Floor
Columbus, OH 43215
(614) 466-5500

Oklahoma
Aging Services Division
Department of Human Services
P.O. Box 25352
Oklahoma City, OK 73125
(405) 521-2327

Oregon
Senior and Disabled Services Division
Department of Human Resources
313 Public Service Building
Salem, OR 97310
(503) 378-4728

Pennsylvania
Pennsylvania Department of Aging
231 State Street
Barto Building
Harrisburg, PA 17101
(717) 783-1550

Rhode Island
Department of Elderly Affairs
160 Pine Street
Providence, RI 02903
(800) 752-8088 (Rhode Island only)
(401) 277-2858

South Carolina
South Carolina Commission on Aging
400 Arbor Lake Drive, Suite B-500
Columbia, SC 29223
(800) 922-1107
(803) 735-0210

South Dakota
Office of Adult Services and Aging
Richard F. Kneip Building
700 Governors Drive
Pierre, SD 57501
(605) 773-3656

Tennessee
Tennessee Commission on Aging
706 Church Street, Suite 201
Nashville, TN 37219
(615) 741-2056

Texas
Texas Department on Aging
P.O. Box 12786
Capitol Station
Austin, TX 78711
(800) 252-9240
(512) 444-2727

Utah
Utah Division of Aging and Adult
  Services
120 North 200 West, Room 4A
P.O. Box 45500
Salt Lake City, UT 84145
(801) 538-3910

Vermont
Department of Rehabilitation and
  Aging
103 South Main Street
Waterbury, VT 05676
(800) 642-5119 (Vermont only)
(802) 241-2400

Virginia
Virginia Department of the Aging
700 East Franklin Street, 10th Floor
Richmond, VA 23219
(800) 552-4464 (Virginia only)
(804) 225-2271

Washington
Aging and Adult Services
  Administration
Department of Social and Health
  Services
Mail Stop OB-44-A
Olympia, WA 98504
(800) 422-3263 (Washington only)
(206) 586-3768

West Virginia
West Virginia Commission on Aging
State Capitol Complex, Holly Grove
1710 Kanawha Boulevard
Charleston, WV 25305
(800) 642-3671 (West Virginia only)
(304) 348-3317

Wisconsin
Bureau on Aging
Department of Health and Social
  Services
1 West Wilson Street, Room 480
P.O. Box 7851
Madison, WI 53707
(608) 266-2536

Wyoming
Commission on Aging
Hathaway Building, 1st Floor
Cheyenne, WY 82002
(307) 777-7986

State Medicare Home-Health Hotlines

Alabama
(800) 356-9596

Alaska
(800) 563-0037

Arizona
(800) 221-9968

Arkansas
(800) 223-0340

California

Berkeley
(800) 554-0352

Chico
(800) 554-0350

Fresno
(800) 554-0351

Sacramento
(800) 554-0354

San Bernardino
(800) 344-2896

San Diego
(800) 824-0613

San Francisco
(800) 554-0353

San Jose
(800) 554-0343

Santa Ana
(800) 228-5234

Santa Rosa
(800) 554-0349

Ventura
(800) 547-8267

Colorado
(800) 842-8826

Connecticut
(800) 828-9769

Delaware
(800) 942-7373

District of Columbia
(800) 727-7873

Florida
(800) 962-6014

Georgia
(800) 869-1150

Hawaii
(800) 548-6577

Idaho
(800) 345-1453

Illinois
(800) 252-4343

Indiana
(800) 227-6334

Iowa
(800) 383-4920

Kansas
(800) 842-0078

Kentucky
(800) 635-6290

Louisiana
(800) 327-3419

Maine
(800) 621-8222

Maryland
(800) 492-6002

Massachusetts
(800) 462-5540

Michigan
(800) 882-6006

Minnesota
(800) 369-7994

Mississippi
(800) 227-7308

Missouri
(800) 877-6485

Montana
(800) 762-4618

Nebraska
(800) 245-5832

Nevada
(800) 225-3414

New Hampshire
(800) 621-6232

New Jersey
(800) 792-9770

New Mexico
(800) 752-8649

New York
(800) 628-5972

North Carolina
(800) 624-3004

North Dakota
(800) 472-2180

Ohio
(800) 342-0553

Oklahoma
(800) 234-7258

Oregon
(800) 542-5186

Pennsylvania
(800) 222-0989

Rhode Island
(800) 228-2716

South Carolina
(800) 922-6735

South Dakota
(800) 592-1861

Tennessee
(800) 541-7367

Texas
(800) 228-1570

Utah
(800) 999-7739

Vermont
(800) 698-4683

Virginia
(800) 955-1819

Washington
(800) 633-6828

West Virginia
(800) 442-2888

Wisconsin
(800) 642-6552

Wyoming
(800) 548-1367

Chapter 9

Print Resources

This chapter includes a supplementary list of books to complement the references found at the end of chapters 1–7.

Alzheimer's Disease, Dementia, and Memory Loss

Dippel, Raye Lynne, and J. Thomas Hutton. *Caring for the Alzheimer Patient: A Practical Guide.* 2nd ed. Buffalo, NY: Prometheus, 1991. 192p. $21.95, $14.95 pa. ISBN 0-87975-662-4, 0-6855-504638 pa.

> A revised and updated edition that includes a chapter on medical breakthroughs, misleading media reports of new research findings, and how to evaluate the reports. The emphasis is on caregiver information on the medical, financial, ethical, and legal aspects of Alzheimer's disease; management of the patient's environment; and available support and coping skills.

Directory of Alzheimer's Disease Treatment Facilities and HomeHealth Care Programs. Baltimore: Health Care Investment Analysts, 1989. 255p. $95.00 ISBN 0-89774-551-5

> The main section lists facilities alphabetically by state with a profile of the facility, its programs, policies, physical setting, and other relevant information. The two indexes are arranged by organization name and a subject classification of programs. The publisher also offers this title on diskette for $399.

Heston, Leonard L., and June A. White. *The Vanishing Mind: A Practical Guide to Alzheimer's Disease and Other Dementias.* New

York: W.H. Freeman, 1991. 192p. $22.95, $13.95 pa. ISBN
0-7167-2131-7, 0-7167-2192-5 pa.

> An extensive revision of the 1983 edition titled *Dementia* with
> new sections on the advances in medical science in understanding
> demential illnesses and the changes in the way our society views
> and approaches dementias. The book presents practical infor-
> mation for families and neighbors on how to react and what to
> expect, information for primary caregivers on what types of care
> are available, and insurance and legal issues. Appendices cover
> tests, associations, and methods of estimating risk for disease
> from known familial factors.

Mace, Nancy, and Peter Rabins. *The Thirty-Six Hour Day: A Family
Guide to Caring for Persons with Alzheimer's Disease, Related
Dementing Illnesses and Memory Loss in Later Life.* Rev. ed.
Baltimore: Johns Hopkins University Press, 1991. 329p. $35.00
ISBN 0-8018-4033-3.

> A compassionate, practical guide for families caring for a person
> with any form of dementia. It details the characteristic social and
> medical problems of both patients and caregivers, where to go
> for outside help, how the caregiver can be helped, and how to get
> through the 36-hour day. One of the best guides for caregivers
> dealing with a form of dementia.

Sheridan, Carmel. *Failure Free Activities for the Alzheimer's Patient.*
San Francisco: Cottage Books, 1987. 104p. $9.95. ISBN 0-943-87305-0.

> A good handbook for caregivers involved in helping anyone
> with a form of dementia, memory loss, or the inability to in-
> terpret everyday happenings. The activities are designed to re-
> inforce the patient's self-esteem and at the same time relieve
> boredom and avoid frustration. There are tables of suggestions
> and computer-generated drawings showing activities, games,
> and projects. Three appendices cover suggested readings, activity
> resources of adaptable children's educational games, and a list
> of organizations that have newsletters and make referrals to
> support groups.

Stewart, Elizabeth. *Tangles of the Mind: A Journey through
Alzheimer's.* Sacramento: Elderberry Press, 1991. 110p. $8.50. ISBN
0-962859-1-9.

A well-written, affectionate portrait of a mother/daughter relationship as the two deal with the confusion, complexities, and losses experienced by both the patient and the caregiver. While Stewart addresses the harsh realities of the disease, the book is not a depressing story of panic and pain.

Assistive Devices, Rehabilitation Aids, Help Books, and Catalogues

Caston, Don. *Eighty-eight Easy To Make Aids for Older People and for Special Needs*. Point Roberts, WA: Hartley & Marks, 1988. 196p. $11.95. ISBN 0-88179-044-3 OP.

> Here are illustrations and step-by-step instructions for easy-to-make aids using basic household tools or sewing equipment and inexpensive materials. Creative ideas for practical aids to help make living more comfortable, safe, and independent. Will also spark ideas for filling specific individual needs.

Living with Low Vision: A Resource Guide for People with Low Vision. Lexington, MA: Resources for Rehabilitation, 1990. 151p. $35. ISBN 0-929718-04-6.

> A large-print comprehensive directory of services, self-help groups, and adaptive technology, including sections on laws that affect those with a vision loss, organizations, special services, and products organized by eye disease. Information is included on sources for talking books and large-print reading materials.

National Stroke Association. *Be Stroke Smart, Adaptive Resources: A Guide to Manufacturers and Products*. 3rd ed. Englewood, CO: National Stroke Association, Jan. 1992. 32p.

> This guide identifies companies that manufacture adaptive equipment, clothing, and other products. Many of the companies listed have brochures or catalogues available at minimal or no cost. While not all-inclusive, this guide has a wealth of valuable information and guidance. For a free copy write to NSA, 300 East Hampden, Suite 240, Englewood, CO 80110-2654, or call (303) 762-9922 or (800) STROKES. Donations to NSA are appreciated.

Remember Catalog. Madison, WI: Bi-Folkal Products, Inc., 1991. 36p.

> Request this free catalogue and receive a complimentary subscription to Bi-Folkal's quarterly newsletter of activity ideas for older people. Write to 809 William Street, Madison, WI 53703. The catalogue offers 16 activity kits on various topics and minikits that create opportunities for older people to remember. They can be used in group settings with other older people, with intergenerational groups, or in a home setting, for both alert and confused older adults. Prices range from $20 to $250. Some components of the kits can be purchased separately. Kits can be rented, and the company sells them to public libraries.

Wilson, Randy. *Non-Chew Cookbook.* Glenwood Springs, CO: Wilson, 1985. 204p. $17.45. ISBN 0-9616299-0-8.

> Published by the author, this cookbook is a collection of 200 recipes he developed for his wife after jaw joint surgery prevented her from chewing for six months. Each recipe has a complete nutritional analysis. The recipes are appealing and can be used for people with chewing disorders or temporary disabilities. The book is wirebound to lay flat, has large print, and is stain- and water-resistant.

Caregiving

Chapman, Elwood N. *The Unfinished Business of Living: Helping Aging Parents Help Themselves.* Los Altos, CA: Crisp, 1987. 256p. $12.95. ISBN 0-931961-19-X.

> This book is directed to the sandwich generation, with the philosophy that when parents receive sensitive and reasonable support everyone in the family benefits. It is well written and organized with worksheets, sample family studies, and exercises. The tone is positive and encouraging, and the worksheets and exercises are easy to use. Not all families are as cooperative and understanding as those in this book, but readers will learn about how to react, interact, and do their best.

Deane, Barbara. *Caring for Your Aging Parents: When Love Is Not Enough.* Colorado Springs: Nava Press, 1989. 267p. $9.95. ISBN 0-89109-578-0.

An informative practical guide by a writer who cofounded Christian Caregivers, a support group for people caring for their elderly parents at home, during her years of caregiving for her elderly mother.

Greenberg, Jerrold S., and others. *The Caregiver's Guide: For Caregivers and the Elderly*. Chicago: Nelson-Hall, 1992. 233p. $25.95, $17.95 pa. ISBN 0-8304-1253-0, 0-8304-1328-6 pa.

A guide to help caregivers learn how to care for themselves along with the caring techniques and medical issues that they need to understand. Emphasis is on how to provide a high quality of life for the caregiver. Appendices include resources and a glossary.

Greenberg, Vivian. *Your Best Is Good Enough*. New York: Lexington, 1989 170p. $16.95. ISBN 0-669-21332-2.

Scenarios presented help caregivers identify with the emotional issues, family relationships, and communication skills of caregiving. The style is informative, understanding, and direct. The book is based on the social work, counseling, and personal experiences of the author. An appendix of resources is included.

Kenny, James, and Stephen Spicer. *Elder Care: Coping with Late-Life Crisis*. Buffalo, NY: Prometheus, 1989. 152p. $13.95. ISBN 0-87975-517-2.

For those who are caregivers now or who may become caregivers or face the responsibilities of making important life choices for those they care for. The book is divided into three parts: preparing for a decision, making a decision, and living with the decision. The authors' approach is realistic, and the language is clear and practical, giving a how-to approach with an understanding of the effort and dedication needed by caregivers.

Koch, Tom. *Mirrored Lives: Aging Children and Elderly Parents*. New York: Praeger, 1990. 217p. $19.95. ISBN 0-275-93671-6.

A son's personal account of his caregiving experience during the geriatric decline of his elderly father due to a nonterminal illness. Through this well-written story, the reader empathizes with the psychological aspects of caregiving for both the son and father and the son's frustrations in giving, finding, and arranging for care. The afterword is a primer on what issues should be discussed and planned before a crisis occurs.

Levin, Nora Jean. *How To Care for Your Parents: A Handbook for Adult Children.* Washington, DC: Storm King Press, 1991. $5.95. ISBN 0-935166-03-3.

> A step-by-step generic manual for organizing the caregiver's time and energy to find resources, get into community resource networks, and become a more effective caregiver. A how-to book written in a concise, cheerful, upbeat style, this is a direct, practical, and easy-to-read elder care resource book.

Niebuhr, Sheryl, and Jane Royse. *Take Care! A Guide for Caregivers on How To Improve Their Self-Care.* St. Paul: Amherst H. Wilder Foundation, 1989. 30p. $2.50.

> In 30 pages this self-help guide is full of practical and proven advice to help caregivers manage stress, cope with negative feelings, learn to relax, ask for help, and more. It encourages caregivers who care to also take care.

Shapiro, Barbara A., and others. *The Big Squeeze: Balancing the Needs of Aging Parents, Dependent Children, and You.* Bedford, MA: Mills & Sanderson, 1991. 228p. $12.95. ISBN 0-938179-29-2.

> Well-organized and written in a positive, you-can-do-it tone, this book offers an eight-step survival plan for dealing with conflicting responsibilities. Good use of anecdotes, hands-on exercises, and commonsense discussions.

Shulman, Bernard, and Reann Berman. *How To Survive Your Aging Parents so You and They Can Enjoy Life.* Chicago: Surrey Books, 1988. 240p. $10.95. ISBN 0-940625-02-4.

> Despite the title, the text focuses on constructive family communication. It answers such important questions for caregivers as, How can I overcome the guilt and anxiety I feel, and Why don't my parents appreciate all that I do for them? This book is for those middle-aged children responsible for the care of elders. The style is relaxed, comforting, and easy to read.

Silverstone, Barbara, and Helen Kandel Hyman. *You and Your Aging Parents: The Family's Guide to Emotional, Physical and Financial Problems.* 3rd ed. New York: Pantheon Books, 1989. 351p. $24.95, $14.95 pa. ISBN 0-394-57741-18, 0-679-72154-1 pa.

The first book that recognized the relationship between the problems of the elderly and the needs of their middle-aged children has been revised to cover the many changes that have occurred since the first edition. It discusses the feelings of both the elderly and the caregivers, how to decide how much help is needed, where to get help, how to be effective caregivers and consumers of services, other aspects of caring for the elderly, and the many life changes that both sides face.

Smith, Kerri S. *Caring for Your Aging Parents: A Sourcebook of Timesaving Techniques and Tips.* Lakewood, CO: American Source Books, 1992. 113p. $8.95. ISBN 0-9621333-8-8.

This volume has eight chapters, each devoted to a specific caregiving concern and ending with a page of Timesavers and a page of Things To Do This Week. This book's arrangement and approach are geared to making organization out of chaos. Appendices include a list of national organizations and a home shopping guide. Useful for all caregivers, not just adult children.

Chronic Illness and Disability

Hutton, J. Thomas, and Raye Lynne Dippel, eds. *Caring for the Parkinson Patient: A Caregiver's Guide.* Buffalo, NY: Prometheus, 1989. 180p. $19.95, $13.95 pa. ISBN 0-87975-478-8, 087975-562-8 pa.

A collection of essays written by professionals who outline their unique therapeutic approaches. The book impresses readers with the necessity of a multidisciplinary approach to dealing with Parkinson's disease. Essays discuss the common problems of Parkinson's, family dynamics, and community support groups. This is essential information and direction for patients and their families.

Levin, Susan B., ed. *Coping with Parkinson's Disease.* St. Louis: American Parkinson's Disease Association. Free booklet with $1.50 for shipping.

A collection of brief discussions by professionals, patients, and family members on various topics relating to coping with Parkinson's in a positive manner.

Maurer, Janet R., and Patricia Strasberg. *Building a New Dream: A Family Guide to Coping with Chronic Illness and Disability*. Reading, MA: Addison-Wesley, 1990. 307p. $9.95. ISBN 0-201-55098-9.

> This book is for families coping with any chronic disease or condition. It deals with nonmedical issues, using vignettes to illustrate common problems or adjustment concerns. Each vignette is followed by specific suggestions.

Financial, Health, Legal, Insurance, and Planning

Abramson, Betsy. *Mastering the Medicare Maze: An Essential Guide to Benefits, Appeals and Medigap Insurance Policies*. Madison, WI: Center for Public Representation, 1991. 144p. $9.95. ISBN 0-932622-40-2.

> This essential guide to benefits, appeals, and Medigap insurance policies written for the layperson includes forms for benefits and appeals with clear instructions for filling them out. A good how-to-do-it guide.

Budish, Armond D. *Avoiding the Medicaid Trap: How To Beat the Catastrophic Costs of Nursing Home Care*. Rev. ed. Salt Lake City: Henry Holt, 1990. 251p. $24.95. ISBN 0-8050-1478-0.

> This book explains strategies for legally protecting savings and assets and using a Medicaid trust. It also includes good advice on legal documents such as a Living Will and a Durable Power of Attorney. The appendices have detachable sample forms for Durable Power of Attorney and model Medicaid trusts. Readers should get competent legal advice on these forms.

Daly, Eugene J. *Thy Will Be Done: A Guide to Wills, Taxation and Estate Planning for Older Persons*. Buffalo, NY: Prometheus, 1990. 230p. $24.95, $16.95 pa. ISBN 0-87975-591-1, 0-87975-586-5 pa.

> A clear guide arranged in four parts, this book discusses wills, estate planning, taxation, executors, and Living Wills. Illustrative examples, sample situations, and a glossary of terms amplify the text.

Dawson, Dolores. *How To Access Medicare—1992*. 3rd ed. Omaha: Dawson Publications, 1991. 155p. $12.95. ISBN 0-962-658-0-7.

An easy-to-read guide that gives the reader a clear, basic understanding of the Medicare program. It includes information on how to file Part A and Part B claims, how to choose supplementary insurance, how to appeal a decision, physician and supplier programs, and other valuable up-to-date information on Medicare. Appendices cover Medicare carriers, state insurance commissioners with toll-free and local telephone numbers, Veterans Administration medical centers, Medicare coverage outside of the United States, and a glossary of Medicare terminology.

Gordon, Haley. *How To Protect Your Life Savings from Catastrophic Illness and Nursing Homes: A Handbook for Financial Survival.* Boston: Financial Planning Institute, 1990. 183p. $19.95. ISBN 0-9625667-0-5.

Written for both a lay audience and professionals who help the elderly and their families, this volume succinctly sets forth the problems of the costs of a chronic illness that leads to long-term care. Gordon's message is not to hide assets but to protect them to the full extent of the law. Scenarios illustrate his points with a discussion of basic strategies, practical advice, and a final section that describes legal instruments.

Jehle, Faustin F. *The Complete and Easy Guide to Social Security and Medicare.* 9th ed. Charlotte, VT: Williamson Publication Co., 1992. 172p. $10.95. ISBN 0-930045-09-2.

This book is revised each year to reflect the changes in effect before the January publication date. The complex information on Social Security, Medicare, disability, and Supplemental Security Income are written in plain English, with charts, examples, sample forms, clear instructions, helpful tips, and pages of sources of information and help.

Polniaszek, Susan. *Long Term Care: A Dollar and Sense Guide.* Washington, DC: United Seniors Health Cooperative, 1991. 64p. $6.95 plus shipping. ISBN 0-944847-03-X.

A comprehensive review of available options with a discussion of resources for living independently and planning for the possibility of nursing home care. Current information on long-term care policies is included. This is a consumer-oriented guide with a open-minded approach.

Polniaszek, Susan. *Managing Your Health Care Finances: Getting the Most out of Medicare and Medigap Insurance*. Rev. ed. Washington, DC: United Seniors Health Cooperative, 1990. 71p. $7.95. ISBN 0-944847-09-0.

> A guide through the health care insurance system. Insurance experts give advice and explain various health insurance programs. Includes systems for organizing medical bills, tracking them through the reimbursement maze, and how to appeal Medicare denials.

Scholen, Ken. *Retirement Income on the House: Cashing in Your Home with a Reverse Mortgage*. Marshall, MN: National Center for Home Equity Conversion Press (NCHEC), 1991. 352p. $24.95. ISBN 0-9630119-6-0.

> A clearly written and comprehensive guide to reverse mortgages by the founder and director of the nonprofit NCHEC. The book is organized into five sections covering how to get started, understanding the basics, analyzing reverse mortgages, reverse mortgage programs, and shopping for reverse mortgages. Three appendices offer more guidance and information. For anyone considering a reverse mortgage now or at some future time.

Van Gelder, Susan, and Diane Johnson. *Long Term Care Insurance: A Market Update*. Washington, DC: Health Insurance Association of America, 1992. 41p. Free booklet.

> An analysis of the long-term care insurance policies sold by 15 companies that represent 75 percent of the 1989 market. A review of services and coverage offered by the leading insurance companies. Lists employers who offered long-term-care insurance in 1990 and a general discussion of employer-sponsored programs. Three appendices with information as of June 1990 on companies and Blue Cross/Blue Shield plans selling long-term-care insurance and companies that offer this insurance as a part of a life insurance policy. Good background information for potential buyers.

Vierck, Elizabeth. *Paying for Health Care after Age 65*. Santa Barbara, CA: ABC-CLIO, 1990. 291p. $45. ISBN 0-87436-095-1.

> Information on health care insurance, managing finances for care, and choosing medical professionals and services. The re-

source section includes a directory of organizations, bibliography of reference works, and a guide to computer-based information.

Health and Home-Care Issues and Planning

Billig, Nathan A. *To Be Old and Sad: Understanding Depression in the Elderly.* New York: Free Press, 1986. 128p. $8.95. ISBN 0-669-12279-3.

> A leading authority on geriatric psychiatry discusses the signs and symptoms of depression, pointing out that depression is not inevitable in the elderly and that it is treatable but must be recognized and diagnosed as depression. There is a guide to the differences between depression and Alzheimer's, Parkinson's, and other diseases, and a section on how medication may cause depression, how to treat a person who does not want help, and available treatments.

Burgio, Kathryn L., and others. *Staying Dry: A Practical Guide to Bladder Control.* Baltimore: Johns Hopkins University Press, 1989. 192p. $26, $12 pa. ISBN 0-8018-3912-2, 0-8018-3909-2 pa.

> Current information about urinary incontinence with a simple five-step program for more effective management of this problem. The book is useful and practical with an extensive glossary.

Golden, Susan. *Nursing a Loved One at Home: A Caregiver's Guide.* Philadelphia: Running Press, 1988. 304p. $33.80, $14.95 pa. ISBN 0-89471-591-7, 0-89471-590-9 pa.

> Written by a registered nurse, the book offers supportive and practical medical information for all levels of care. The author has anticipated caregivers' problems, worries, and questions. Each chapter ends with a caregiver's checklist. There are over 55 line drawings, charts, and appendices of weights and measures, resources, suggested readings, and a glossary of technical terms.

Hinrichsen, Gregory A. *Mental Health Problems and Older Adults.* Santa Barbara, CA: ABC-CLIO, 1990. 300p. $45.00. ISBN 0-87436-240-7.

> Written for a knowledgeable audience, the first section presents an overview of the mental health problems with case studies. The

second section has listings of resources, mental health organizations, books, films, and videocassettes.

Lewis, Carole B., and Linda C. Campanelli. *Health Promotion and Exercise for Older Adults: An Instruction Guide.* Aspen Series in Physical Therapy. Rockville, MD: Aspen Publications, 1990. 192p. $39. ISBN 0-8342-0169-0.

> A practical, how-to exercise manual developed for the nonprofessional. It contains practical background information, and each chapter addresses a particular area in a step-by-step approach. Clear instructions and illustrations.

Lorig, Kate, and James F. Fries. *The Arthritis Handbook.* 3rd ed. Reading, MA: Addison-Wesley, 1990. 266p. $ 10.95. ISBN 0-201-52403-1.

> Recommended by the Arthritis Foundation, this handbook is clearly and simply written with charts and illustrations of exercises and devices.

Rob, Caroline, and Janet Reynolds. *The Caregiver's Guide: Helping Elderly Relatives Cope with Health and Safety Problems.* Boston: Houghton Mifflin, 1991. 458p. $22.95. ISBN 0-395-50086-9.

> Fourteen chapters on specific health problems and issues clearly explain each disease, symptoms, progression, medical and nursing procedures, and everything a caregiver needs to know to be competent and knowledgeable. Appendices list help and resources.

Thornton, Howard A. *A Medical Handbook for Senior Citizens and Their Families.* Westport, CT: Greenwood, 1989. 400p. $45, $16.95 pa. ISBN 0-86569-171-1, 0-086569-175-4 pa.

> Well-written in a clear, practical, and thorough manner for individuals, families, and professionals, this book presents information on common and uncommon health problems, prevention and treatment procedures, and health-related matters that cause a great deal of emotional stress in families. It contains lists of tests, medications and their side effects, charts, and other specialized sections on diseases and health consumer information.

Housing Options

Down, Ivy M., and Lorraine Schnurr. *Between Home and Nursing Home: The Board and Care Alternative*. Buffalo, NY: Prometheus, 1991. 210p. $18.95, $13.95 pa. ISBN 0-87975-619-5, 0-87975-620-9 pa.

> This a guide on how to locate and choose a board and care home, with checklists and information on long-term care ombudsmen. This book has suggestions and advice for those who manage board and care homes, older people, and caregivers who are considering one.

Gillespie, Ann E., and Katrinka Smith Sloan. *Housing Options and Services for Older Adults*. Santa Barbara, CA: ABC-CLIO, 1990. 279p. $45. ISBN 0-87436-144-3.

> A reference book on the variety of housing options and services available for the older adult. It is divided into two sections, a narrative and an annotated resource section with bibliography, directory of organizations, and glossary.

National Consumers League. *Consumer's Guide to Life-Care Communities*. Washington, DC: National Consumers League, 1990. 27p. $4 for nonmembers, $2 for NCL members.

> A consumer-oriented, concise guide for the evaluation of life-care communities, how to make on-site visits, financial risks, and a four-page checklist of questions.

Medications

Anderson, Kenneth, and Lois Anderson. *Orphan Drugs*. New York: Putnam, 1987. 253p. ISBN 0-895-866-43-9.

> This volume catalogues more than 1,500 generic and brand name drugs that have been scientifically tested and licensed in foreign countries to treat more than 800 maladies and diseases. It includes a symptoms directory, index of drug names, and a source directory of more than 200 drug companies.

Silverman, Harold. *The Pill Book for Senior Citizens*. New York: Bantam Books, 1989. 320p. $5.50. ISBN 0-553-25660-2.

The book presents descriptions and information on the medications most often prescribed for the senior population. It is clearly written to educate and help readers understand how to take medications and avoid drug interactions.

U.S. Pharmacopoeia. *The Complete Drug Reference*. Yonkers, NY: Consumer Report Books, 1992. 1,321p. $39.95 ISBN 0-89043-479-4.

The first section contains articles on the correct use of any medicine, followed by an alphabetical listing of drug monographs with clearly written descriptions of how to take the drug properly, side effects, precautions, generic and trade names, and uses. An appendix of life-sized color photographs of most frequently prescribed medications is included. More than 5,500 prescribed and over-the-counter drugs are profiled in a clear, easy-to-understand manner by an unbiased, independent source.

Reference Materials

Case Management Resource Guide: 1992 ed. Irvine, CA: Center for Consumer Healthcare Information, 1992. 4-vol. set. $225 plus shipping. ISBN 0-1-880874-00-8. Individual regional volumes, $60 plus shipping. Vol. 1, Eastern, ISBN 1-880874-01-06; Vol. 2, Southern, ISBN 1-880874-02-4; Vol. 3, Midwestern, ISBN 1-880874-03-2; Vol. 4, Western, ISBN 1-880874-04-0.

The four regional volumes contain more than 70,000 entries on health-care services and facilities with detailed information. More than 50 categories of health care resources and specialized resources are listed. Entries include contact names, services, phone numbers, addresses, affiliations, and other pertinent information. Available in hardcopy and electronic formats, and updated annually.

Directory of Nursing Homes. 5th ed. 1991-1992. Baltimore: Health Care Investment Analysts, 1991. 1,479p. $225. Diskette $2500. ISBN 0-89774-665-1.

An introduction on long-term care insurance is followed by alphabetical listings by state and city of more than 16,000 licensed facilities in the United States, Puerto Rico, and the Virgin Islands. Lists name, address, telephone number, number of beds, level of care, and Medicare and Medicaid certification. For some facilities, additional information is given on languages spoken, number of full- and part-time staff, special facilities, or activities. Three indexes list nursing homes by affiliation, alphabetically by state and county, and corporate nursing home headquarters.

Donavin, Denise Perry. *Aging with Style and Savvy: Books and Films on Challenges Facing Adults of All Ages.* Chicago: American Library Association. 270p. $25. ISBN 0-8389-0526-9.

> Reviews of novels, biographies, nonfiction works, videos, films, and plays that deal with the needs of adults over 50 and the younger adults who are involved with them. The titles reviewed present issues and useful information on aging, or are works of literature that challenge society's negative stereotypes of the elderly.

Elder Services 1992–1993: The Greater Chicago Area Guide to Elder-care. Phoenix: Oryx Press, 1992. 392p. $14.95. ISBN 0-89774-664-3.

Elder Services 1991–1992: Los Angeles County Guide. Phoenix: Oryx Press, 1991. 301p. $14.95. ISBN 0-89774-663-5.

> This is a series of guides to services for the elderly in large metropolitan areas for family caregivers, social service, and health care professionals. Practical advice and information by local experts are followed by lists of organizations, helpful materials, and helplines. Checklists for selecting services and nursing homes and detailed directories of facilities arranged by geographic areas are featured. Directories covering approximately 20 other urban areas such as Dallas and San Francisco will be published by Health Care Investment Analysts (HCIA) of Baltimore, which plans to publish six to eight directories a year.

Resources for Rehabilitation. *Rehabilitation Resource Manual: Vision.* 3rd ed. Lexington, MA: Resources for Rehabilitation, 1990. 1151p. $39.95 ISBN 0-929718-05-4.

> Descriptions of services, products, and publications to help people with disabilities function independently. Sections cover laws that affect elders with disabilities, organizations, professional service providers, special equipment and assistive devices, and specific losses. Book is in large print.

U.S. National Institute on Aging. *Resource Directory for Older People.* Bethesda, MD: National Institute on Aging, 1991. 224p.

> For one free copy send a postcard to the NIA Information Center, Directory, P.O. Box 8057, Gaithersburg, MD 20898-8057. The directory contains an alphabetical listing of more than 180 agencies serving older people. For each listing there is a detailed mission statement and information on services and publications.

Reminiscing

American Association of Retired Persons (AARP). *Reminiscence: Reaching Back, Moving Forward.* Washington, DC: AARP. AARP fulfillment publication no. D13186. Free.

> This publication describes the values and techniques of reminiscence with questions and triggers to help the person remember and lists of resources for reminiscence activities.

Rosenbluth, Vera. *Keeping Family Stories Alive: A Creative Guide to Taping Your Family Life and Lore.* Point Roberts, WA: Hartley & Marks, 1990. 175p. $14.95. ISBN 0-88179-026-5.

> This book includes new material on memory and advice on how to jog memories for both the interviewer and the interviewee. Instructions are simple and direct, based on the author's career of producing family documents for clients, and include advice on how to handle microphones, audiotape, and videotape, and how to preserve and use the tapes.

Sheridan, Carmel. *Reminiscence: The Key to Healthy Aging.* San Francisco: Cottage Books, 1991. 164p. $11.95. ISBN 0-943873-10-X.

> A clear, practical guide for use in the home by family and friends or by professionals in hospitals, nursing homes, or day-care centers. The book is divided into two sections, the first on themes and memory makers, the second on reminiscing activities. Covered are how to tape or write a life story, arts and crafts, and reminiscing with specific groups and items. There are ten appendices of resources for reminiscence and a short index.

Thorsheim, Howard I., and Bruce B. Roberts. *Reminiscing Together: Ways To Help Us Keep Mentally Fit as We Grow Older.* Minneapolis: Comp-Care, 1990. 143p. $7.95. ISBN 0-8938-221-4.

Written by two psychology professors, this is a guide on how to share life stories with family and friends, improve short- and long-term memory, and stimulate the memory through the senses. Memory strengthening exercises are included. A large-print book.

Newsletters

Aging Network News
P.O. Box 1233
McLean, VA 22101
(703) 734-3266

> Articles on all aspects of aging, including legislation, innovative programs, and services.

Aging Research and Training News
Business Publishing Inc.
951 Pershing Drive
Silver Spring, MD 20910-4464
(301) 587-6300

> Published 22 times a year for professionals in the field of aging, this newsletter covers federal and state programs, congressional action, research aspects of aging, and training for professionals in the field. Subscription basis.

Be Stroke Smart
National Stroke Association
1420 Ogden Street
Denver, CO 80218
(303) 762-9922
(800)-STROKES

> Free quarterly publication dealing with news summaries, helpful information, and membership news.

The Capsule
Children of Aging Parents
1609 Woodbourne Road, Suite 302A
Levittown, PA 19057
(215) 945-6900

> Bimonthly publication dealing with caregiver issues, personal experiences, news, and book reviews. Comes with yearly membership.

The Caregiver
Duke Family Support Program
P.O. Box 3600
Duke Medical Center
Durham, NC 27710
(919) 684-2328
(800) 672-4213 (North Carolina residents only)

> A quarterly newsletter for both professionals and family care-
> givers of persons with Alzheimer's Disease. Free to families in
> North Carolina with a $10 subscription rate for those outside of
> North Carolina.

Caregiver News
106 Lowell Street
Manchester, NH 03101

> This quarterly newsletter is published by an interfaith volunteer
> coalition.

Caregivers Quarterly
National Federation of Interfaith Volunteer Caregivers, Inc.
P.O. Box 1939
Kingston, NY 12401
(914) 331-1358

> Quarterly newsletter of the religious network of voluntary care-
> giver programs.

Caregiving
Caregiver Support Program
Bloomington Hospital Senior Health Services
P.O. Box 1149
Bloomington, IN 47402
(812) 336-9300

> Monthly newsletter that provides information, education, and
> news for caregivers with a regional emphasis serving south cen-
> tral Indiana.

Caregiving News
Case Western Reserve University
Mandel School of Applied Social Sciences
11235 Bellflower Road
Cleveland, OH 44106-7164
(213) 368-2290

The newsletter published by the Family Caregiving Project
for professional caregivers also contains useful information for
family members.

Chronic Pain Letter
Dolak Inc.
P.O. Box 1303
Old Chelsea Station, NY 10011
(718) 797-0015

> Bimonthly with current information on the management of
> chronic pain for both patients and health professionals. Contains
> abstracts of relevent articles from a wide range of journals and
> original articles of interest to the general chronic pain specialties.
> By subscription: $35 for professionals and institutions, $20 for
> the general reader.

Co-Op Network
Mercy Family Practice Center
St. John's Mercy Medical Center
615 South New Ballas Road
St. Louis, MO 63141

> The bimonthly newsletter of Caregivers of Older Persons, a care-
> giver support network in Missouri.

Elderly Health Services Letter
American Resources Publishing
3100 Highway 138, Box 1442
Wall Township, NJ 07719
(908) 681-1133

> A monthly newsletter for professionals, with information on
> trends and developments in the field of health services for the
> elderly.

Heart, Health, Education and Aging: Resources for Training
Geriatric Education Center of PA
Temple University, Institute On Aging
1601 North Broad Street
Philadelphia, PA 19122
(215) 787-65834

> Biannual publication highlighting resources for training for
> professionals.

HIP, Inc.
Help for Incontinent People
Box 544
Union, SC 29379
(803) 579-7900

> A quarterly publication with information and resources on the loss of bladder control, treatment options, and referrals to other sources of information.

Human Values and Aging Newsletter
Brookdale Center on Aging
Hunter College
425 East 25th Street
New York, NY 10010-2590
(212) 481-4353

> A bimonthly newsletter for professionals in the aging field dealing with current information on aging research, legal issues, government policies, and senior rights.

The Informer: Helping People with Incontinence
The Simon Foundation
P.O. Box 815
Wilmette, IL 60091
(800) 237-4666
(708) 864-3913

> Quarterly newsletter of medical articles, helpful devices, and publications on incontinence. Also has a pen pal list. It comes with membership in the Simon Foundation.

Kinship
P.O. Box 10433
Denver, CO 80210
> Statewide membership organization newsletter for families of nursing home residents.

New York State Office for the Aging Newsletter
New York State Office for the Aging
Empire State Plaza
Albany, NY 12223
(518) 474-7181

A free bimonthly newsletter devoted to issues of aging, the aged, and those concerned with caring for the aged.

Northwest Caregiver
Education and Family Support Services
Neurological Sciences Center
Good Samaritan Hospital and Medical Center
1015 Northwest 22nd Street
Portland, OR 97210-5198

> A quarterly newsletter for caregivers and professionals dealing with caring issues, problems, and solutions, published by the Care Club of the hospital.

Older Americans Report
Business Publishing Inc.
951 Pershing Drive
Silver Spring, MD 20910-4464
(301) 587-6300

> Published weekly, focusing on services to the elderly, covers federal and state programs, and congressional action designed for service providers and professionals working in the aging field. Subscription basis.

Senior Care Professionals
CD Publications
8024 Fenton Street
Silver Spring, MD 20910
(301) 588-6380

> Bimonthly reports for senior care professionals.

SHHH, A Journal about Hearing Loss
Self-Help for Hard of Hearing People
7800 Wisconsin Avenue
Bethesda, MD 20814
(301) 657-2248 (voice)
(301) 657-2249 (TDD)

> The journal is a bimonthly publication with information on hearing impairments, community resources, coping with hearing loss, and other relevant topics.

Well Spouse Newsletter
Well Spouse Foundation
P.O. Box 28876
San Diego, CA 92198-0876
(619) 673-9043

> Newsletter for membership, which is open to any well spouse of someone who is chronically ill. There are local self-help support groups. The newsletter offers information on emotional support, insurance coverage, new programs to help families deal with chronic illness, parenting concerns, and other topics.

Chapter 10

Nonprint Resources

Audiovisual

Alzheimer's Disease and Other Dementias

Designing the Physical Environment for Persons with Dementia

Type: Slides and Videocassette, 1/2″ VHS

Length: 20 min.

Cost: Slide purchase $175, plus $7 shipping and handling; video-cassette $110, plus $7 shipping and handling; rental $45 (video only), plus $7 shipping and handling.

Source: Producer, University of Michigan, Institute of Gerentology
Distributor, Terra Nova Films, Inc.
9848 South Winchester Avenue
Chicago, IL 60643
(312) 881-8491

Date: 1987

This video is based on the results of a demonstration project called Wesley Hall, a special dementia unit at the University of Michigan designed to create a warm, stimulating, and supportive environment that would enhance the lives of the residents. Eleven key factors in planning such an environment are described; stimulation for the senses and cues for orientation, uses of colors and lighting, correct signage, safety measures, and other useful design elements are shown. Helpful for caregivers in evaluating how to make their residences safer and easier for their care recipient.

No Easy Answer and A Delicate Balance

Type: Videocassette, 1/2″ VHS
Length: 29 min. and 20 min.
Cost: $26 for both videos
Source: Metro Home for the Aged
          14th Floor, East Tower, City Hall
          Toronto, Ontario, Canada M5H2N1
          (416) 392-8928
Date: 1990

> These two videos provide practical information for family members who care for elderly relatives with Alzheimer's disease. *No Easy Answer* has discussions on the changes of behavior and the ways in which caregivers must relate and adapt through an interchange with various professionals. *A Delicate Balance* gives very good practical suggestions for safety measures and sensitization to potentially dangerous physical arrangements in a residence. Together they can help the caregiver carry out tasks of daily living.

Not Alone Anymore

Type: Videocassette, 1/2″ VHS
Length: 22 min.
Cost: Purchase $195, plus $7 shipping and handling; rental $55, plus $7.00 for shipping and handling.
Source: Terra Nova Films, Inc.
          9848 South Winchester Avenue
          Chicago, IL 60643
          (312) 881-8491
Date: 1989

> Based on the real-life experiences of caregivers of family members with Alzheimer's disease, this video presents helpful, down-to-earth information, guidelines, and strategies on both caregiving and how to care for oneself as a caregiver. Accurate and practical suggestions are geared directly to the caregiver.

Caregivers and Caregiving Issues

Before the Going Gets Rough
(Part 1 of a two-part program called Prevention and Management of Aggressive Behavior in the Elderly)

Type: Videocassette, 1/2", 3/4" VHS
Length: 30 min.
Cost: Purchase $250, rental $100 for both parts
Source: Good Samaritan Hospital & Medical Center
          Family Support Center
          1015 NW 22nd Avenue
          Portland, OR 97210-5198
          (503) 229-7348
Date: 1988

> A group of caregivers share their experiences with two nurses as the group leaders, including the stresses the caregivers feel and how they manage and defuse care recipients' aggressive behavior. A geriatrician and a nurse describe age-related changes and other events that cause disruption. The two segments offer information and comfort to viewers, reminding them they are not alone and showing how to understand and deal with their problems.

How To Find and Evaluate High Quality Eldercare
Type: Videocassette, 1/2", 3/4", VHS
Length: 42 min.
Cost: Purchase $500, no rental.
Source: Dependent Care Connection
          P.O. Box 2783
          Westport, CT 06880
          (203) 226-2680
Date: 1987

> This information is for the sandwich generation of caregivers with both child care and elder care responsibilities. The important facets of elder care are presented, and housing options for the elderly are categorized. An empathetic approach to the difficulties of being a caregiver with practical assistance in choosing a good care plan for a frail older relative.

In Care of: Families and Their Elders
Type: Videocassette, 1/2" VHS, 3/4" U-matic
Length: 55 min.
Cost: 1/2" VHS purchase $295, 3/4" U-matic $345, rental $50
Source: Producer, Menachem Daum
          Distributor, Brookdale Center on Aging of Hunter College

425 East 25th Street
New York, NY 10010
(212) 481-7550
(800) 648-COPE outside New York state

Date: 1988

Real family members and their care recipients were filmed in their own homes in working-class neighborhoods in New York's outer boroughs as they struggled and coped with the physical, emotional, and financial challenges of caregiving. Through the video, families are given needed skills and information along with help in coming to terms with their feelings. There are two short segments on geriatric medicine and congregate living. A discussion guide accompanies the video.

My Mother, My Father

Type: Film, 16mm, or videocassette, 1/2" VHS
Length: 33 min.
Cost: Film purchase $495; videocassette purchase $335, plus $7 shipping and handling; videocassette rental $55, plus $7 shipping and handling.
Source: Terra Nova Films, Inc.
         9848 South Winchester Avenue
         Chicago, IL 60643
         (312) 881-8491
Date: 1985

A candid look at four families and their mixed feelings as they deal with the stresses of the caregivers for aging parents. The film does not attempt to give answers but gives viewers a better understanding of the issues confronting the families. A 16-page discussion guide is included.

My Mother, My Father: Seven Years Later

Type: Videocassette, 1/2" VHS
Length: 42 min.
Cost: Purchase $335, plus $7 shipping and handling; rental $55, plus $7 shipping and handling.
Source: Terra Nova Films, Inc.
         9848 South Winchester Avenue
         Chicago, IL 60643
         (312) 881-8491
Date: 1991

This sequel is as effective and stimulating as the original. It brings the viewer up to date on the status of the caregivers and care receivers. It shows what aspects of the caregiving relationships have been resolved over the seven years, what aspects have been left unresolved, and what new conflicts have come about. A major theme is that caregiving is the catalyst for resolving long-standing family conflicts. The original film and the sequel, when viewed together, reinforce that caregiving is a process that changes over time as do caregivers.

On the Aging of Parents . . . Closing the Gap

Type: Videocassette, 1/2″ VHS
Length: 18 min.
Cost: Purchase $49.95, no rental.
Source: Lutheran Center on Aging
           911 Stewart
           Seattle, WA 98103
           (206) 467-6532
Date: 1984

Uses six professionally acted dramas to give the viewer instant identification of the communication difficulties between generations. Topics range from coping with a confused older parent to generational stereotypes to the stresses of three generations living together. Self-study booklet that accompanies the tape acts as a resource guide.

On the Aging of Parents . . . A Guide for Adult Children

Type: Videocassette, 1/2″ VHS
Length: 4–5 hours of programming with leader's guide. Leader can control length of each minidrama.
Cost: Purchase $49.95, no rental
Source: Lutheran Center on Aging
           911 Stewart
           Seattle, WA 98103
           (206) 467-6532
Date: 1984

Provides an introductory survey of real-life issues confronting the elderly and their children. Seven minidramas enact issues ranging from children's denial of their parents' aging to dealing with a parent's unsafe driving. Each minidrama is followed by questions for discussion. Leader's guide accompanies the video.

On the Aging of Parents . . . Love Can Hurt

Type: Videocassette, 1/2" VHS
Length: 4−5 hours of programming with leader's guide. Leader can control length of each minidrama.
Cost: Purchase $49.95, no rental
Source: Lutheran Center on Aging
         911 Stewart
         Seattle, WA 98103
         (206) 467-6532
Date: 1984

Seven minidramas look at aging from a family perspective, dealing with wills, power of attorney, nursing home placement, sibling rivalry, long-distance relationships, neighbors as family, and more.

Respite: Taking Care

Type: Videocassette, 1/2", 3/4" VHS
Length: 21 min.
Cost: Purchase $195, rental $50/day, $100/week
Source: Producer, Jane Feinberg
         Distributor, Fanlight Productions
         47 Halifax Street
         Boston, MA 02130
         (617) 524-0980
Date: 1990

Profiles of four families show the physical and emotional stresses of caregiving. Options for respite for caregivers are shown, along with the positive role of a caregivers' support group. The families interviewed are of different races and ages.

Sharing the Challenge of Aging

Type: Slide-tape
Length: 12 min.
Cost: Purchase $72 plus $3 shipping and handling
Source: Potentials Development for Health and Aging Services
         775 Main Street, Suite 321
         Buffalo, NY 14203-1387
Date: 1985

Based on real situations of older people and their families, this production raises questions and issues for group discussion. Focus is on the changes that come with the aging process and the benefits that each generation can get from positive interaction. Issues include how can the two generations live together; how can families best meet the special needs of a frail elderly relative; and delicate problems such as stopping driving, remarriage, sharing activities, and more. While the tone is encouraging and positive, the need to prepare is emphasized. A leader's guide provides suggestions for how to use this slide-tape with groups, lists of issues and discussion questions, and the complete slide-tape script.

Exercise, Stress, and Wellness

Armchair Fitness: A Home Aerobic Workout
Type: Videocassette, 1/2" VHS
Length: 60 min.
Cost: Purchase $39.95 each, plus $2.50 shipping and handling; no rental
Source: CC-M Productions
           8510 Cedar Street
           Silver Spring, MD 20910
           (301) 588-4095
Date: 1986

Designed to be an aerobic workout performed in a chair, this video presents three 20-minute group exercise sessions, increasing in vigor. Big band music sets a lively pace. The participants use their muscles to improve circulation, flexibility, coordination, and general well-being.

Arthritis Exercises
Type: Videocassette, 1/2" VHS
Length: 35 min.
Cost: Purchase $79.95, plus $7 shipping and handling; no rental
Source: Terra Nova Films, Inc.
           9848 South Winchester Avenue
           Chicago, IL 60643
           (312) 881-8491
Date: 1987

This gentle exercise program for people affected by arthritis and related joint stiffness can also be used as a low-impact workout for any older adult. Exercises are demonstrated slowly and are easy to follow. The video can be used at home by single viewers or in a group setting.

Elderly Rhythms

Type:	Videocassette, 1/2", 3/4" VHS
Length:	18 min.
Cost:	Purchase $295, plus $5 shipping and handling; rental $60, plus $5 shipping and handling
Source:	Fairview Audiovisuals 17909 Groveland Avenue Cleveland, OH 44111 (216) 476-7054
Date:	1984

An exercise program for the well elderly presented in a low-key, warm manner with clear verbal and visual instructions and unobtrusive background music.

Fitness over 50

Type:	Videocassette, 1/2" VHS
Length:	Two 50-min. segments
Cost:	Purchase $39.95, plus $3.50 shipping and handling; no rental
Source:	Health Tapes, Inc. 13320 North End Oak Park, MI 48237 (313) 548-2500
Date:	1986

The first of two separate low-impact exercise programs is for beginners, the second for those more advanced. Both parts are for older persons and anyone overweight, sedentary, or just beginning an exercise program. The objective is to improve the participant's strength, flexibility, energy level, and muscle tone. The exercises are designed to protect the weight-bearing joints.

Get Up and Go With Parkinson's

Type:	Videocassette, 1/2" VHS
Length:	60 min.

Cost: Purchase $42.95, plus $3.50 shipping and handling; no rental
Source: Health Tapes, Inc.
           13320 North End
           Oak Park, MI 48237
           (313) 548-2500
Date: 1989

These exercises for people with Parkinson's disease are to be used in conjunction with prescribed medical treatment. This new dimension in the treatment of Parkinson's must be reviewed with the patient's physician and medical advisors before the patient tries the exercises.

Financial, Insurance, and Legal Issues

Can't Afford To Grow Old
Type: Videocassette, 1/2″ VHS
Length: 55 min.
Cost: Purchase $395, plus $7 shipping and handling, rental $75, plus $7 shipping and handling
Source: Producer, Roger Weisberg
           Distributor, Filmmakers Library
           124 East 40th Street
           New York, NY 10016
           (212) 808-4980
           Distributor, Terra Nova Films, Inc.
           9848 South Winchester Avenue
           Chicago, IL 60643
           (312) 881-8491
Date: 1989

An informative and thought-provoking presentation of long-term care issues from the expert's, caregiver's, and care receiver's perspectives. Pros and cons are given on universal government-financed long-term care, private insurance, and use of family assets. Case studies that illustrate the issues are followed by commentary. While the segment on the Catastrophic Health Care Medicare Amendment is now obsolete, it reinforces the point that the major long-term care issues were not addressed by the amendment. Hosted and narrated by Walter Cronkite.

The Coming of Age in America

Type: Videocassette, 1/2" VHS
Length: 30 min.
Cost: Purchase $24.95; no rental
Source: Producer, John Hancock Financial Services
           Distributor, National Council on the Aging
           Dept. 5087
           Washington, DC 20061-5087
           (202) 479-1200
Date: 1988

Narrated by Willard Scott, this video introduces background material and conducts a solid discussion on the country's long-term care issues. There are clear explanations of the demographic, family, and financial trends that have an impact on the long-term care dilemma the country faces as the population ages.

The Cost of Caring

Type: Videocassette, 1/2",3/4" VHS
Length: 28 min.
Cost: Purchase 3/4", $49; 1/2", $29.95; no rental
Source: Producer, Steven Talley
           Distributor, KCET Video
           4401 Sunset Boulevard
           Los Angeles, CA 90027
           (213) 668-9541
Date: 1988

This documentary produced for public television discusses the financial burden of long-term care for the elderly by dramatizing the experiences of three married couples in which the husbands require long-term care. While the information on Medicaid and federal laws has changed, the issues and the emotional trauma portrayed are still relevant. The video includes actual caregiving scenes as well as interviews with the families and professionals.

Health, Home Care, and Safety

Coping and Home Safety Tips for Caregivers of the Elderly

Type: Videocassette, 1/2" VHS
Length: 17 min.

Cost: Purchase $89.95 (video and manual), $9.95 (manual alone)
Source: JABA Video
           2300 Commonwealth Drive, Suite B-1
           Charlottesville, VA 22901
Date: 1987

Practical information, full of helpful tips for caregivers, affordable ideas to meet the special needs of caring at home, demonstrations on adaptive equipment, and ways to make simple, low-cost changes to lessen the risk of accidents. The manual can be used independently.

Overmedicating the Elderly

Type: Videocassette, 1/2″ VHS
Length: 28 min.
Cost: Purchase $149, plus 5 percent shipping and handling; rental $75, plus 5 percent shipping and handling
Source: Producer, Multimedia Entertainment Inc.
           Distributor, Films for the Humanities and Sciences, Inc.
           P.O. Box 2053
           Princeton, NJ 08543
           (800) 257-5126
Date: 1990

This segment of "Donahue" features Dr. Sidney Wolfe, author of *Worst Pills, Best Pills*. Using the case study format, older adults review their routine medications, and Dr. Wolfe explains that older adults are more susceptible to adverse drug reactions and gives a list of ten rules for safe drug use. Much valuable information is covered.

Safety for Seniors

Type: Film (16mm) and videocassette, 1/2″, 3/4″ VHS
Length: 23 min.
Cost: Purchase $450 (16mm and 3/4″ video), $400 (1/2″ video); rental $45 (16mm), $40 (1/2″ and 3/4″ video)
Source: Handel Film Corporation
           8730 Sunset Boulevard
           Los Angeles, CA 90069
           (213) 657-8990
Date: 1985

A how-to video that teaches older consumers to recognize and eliminate hazards in the home. The safety measures shown are simple and can be implemented with little or no cost. While intended for the older person, children of aging parents and others can benefit as well.

Long-Term Care

A Family Decision

Type: Videocassette, 1/2″ VHS
Length: 25 min.
Cost: Purchase $245, plus $7 shipping and handling; rental $45, plus $7 shipping and handling
Source: Producer, American Medical Services
            Distributor, Terra Nova Films, Inc.
            9848 South Winchester Avenue
            Chicago, IL 60643
            (312) 881-8491
Date: 1985

This presentation focuses on the emotional difficulties of a nursing home placement. Family members openly discuss the experiences and feelings that occurred in their decision-making process.

A New Home

Type: Videocassette, 1/2″ VHS
Length: 28 min.
Cost: Purchase $150, plus $7 shipping and handling; rental $55, plus $7 shipping and handling
Source: Producer, Mature Market Productions
            Distributor, Terra Nova Films, Inc.
            9848 South Winchester Avenue
            Chicago, IL 60643
            (312) 881-8491
Date: 1991

Four families from different backgrounds openly discuss their experiences in placing a family member in a long-term care facility. Three parts cover making the decision, admission and initial adjustment, and ongoing coping. The latter deals with visits, roommates, other family members, laundry, and emotional reactions.

One East
Type: Videocassette, 1/2″, 3/4″ VHS
Length: 28 min.
Cost: Purchase $400, rental $100
Source: Video Press
           The University of Maryland at Baltimore
           School of Medicine
           32 South Greene Street
           Baltimore, MD 21201
           (410) 328-5497
Date: 1991

> A balanced portrayal of the good and bad, happy and sad, normal and unusual events of everyday life in a nursing home in a slice of life style. For family members this serves as a starting point for identifying fears and misconceptions and developing criteria for evaluating and selecting a nursing home.

Specific Illnesses

Aphasia: My Life in the Mists
Type: Audiocassette
Length: 37 min.
Cost: Purchase $9.95
Source: Duvall Media, Inc.
           P.O. Box 15892
           Newport Beach, CA 92659-5892
           (800) 726-3465
Date: 1991

> Rosemary Collett tells of her recovery, one step at a time, from a stroke. Five years later, she lectures to caregivers and health professionals about the effects of and reactions to aphasia. Informative and helpful for stroke patients and their families and friends.

Family Business: Living with Heart Disease
Type: Videocassette, 1/2″ VHS
Length: 47 min.
Cost: Purchase $150, plus $12 shipping and handling; rental $75, plus $12 shipping and handling

Source: The Living Series
           c/o Video Catalog
           561 Broadway
           New York, NY 10012
           (212) 274-1867
Date: 1988

Seven heart patients and their families share their struggles, challenges, and successes. These are positive role models who have learned to make responsible choices about attitudes, activities, and medical care. Their ages range from 49 to 75, and their stories have much to offer heart patients and their families.

Have You Heard?
Type: Videocassette, 1/2″ VHS, and booklet
Length: 15 min.
Cost: Purchase $20, rental free for programs
Source: AARP A/V Programs
           P.O. Box 20049, Station R
           Washington, DC 20036
           (202) 434-6115
Date: Unavailable

Information on the identification, treatment, and potential for correcting hearing problems in the elderly, as well as when and where to get a hearing aid and how to cope with a hearing loss.

The Healing Influence: Guidelines for Stroke Families
Type: Videocassette, 1/2″, 3/4″ VHS
Length: 43 min.
Cost: Purchase $299 (1/2″), $399 (3/4″), plus $5 shipping and handling for any purchase; rental $55
Source: Danamar Productions
           106 Monte Vista Place
           Santa Fe, NM 87501
           (505) 986-9072
Date: 1990

This sensitive and powerful documentary interweaves true stories told by stroke survivors with the reactions and feelings expressed by their families. They provide true-to-life descriptions, explanations, and examples of a gamut of emotions. In addition there are discussions and insights from doctors and other health professionals on healing and rehabilitation.

Parkinson's Disease: How To Cope and Live with It

Type: Audiocassette
Length: 47 min.
Cost: Purchase $9.95
Source: Duvall Media, Inc.
         P.O. Box 15892
         Newport Beach, CA 92659-5892
         (800) 726-3465
Date: 1991

> Written by a Parkinson's disease patient, this personal account offers a good layperson's explanation of the disorder and many of its common problems such as swallowing and walking, as well as his suggestions for coping with courage, good humor, and a positive outlook.

A Personal Challenge: Living with Arthritis

Type: Videocassette, $1/2''$ VHS
Length: 37 min.
Cost: Purchase $150, plus $12 shipping and handling; rental $75, plus $12 shipping and handling
Source: The Living Series
         c/o Video Catalog
         561 Broadway
         New York, NY 10012
         (212) 274-1867
Date: 1988

> A sensitive portrayal of six people learning to adapt, understand, make choices, deal with their pain, and meet the challenges of living with arthritis. Ages range from 26 to 86; their stories are helpful to patients and their families.

Databases

Abeldata
National Rehabilitation Information Center (NARIC)
8455 Colesville Road
Silver Spring, MD 20910-3319
(800) 346-2742 (voice and TDD)

> Abeldata is an information source funded by the National Institute on Disability and Rehabilitation Research of the U.S.

Department of Education and maintained by the Adaptive Equipment Center of Newington Children's Hospital, Newington, Connecticut, and is the largest source in the nation on disability-related products. Abeldata is a continually updated product database with more than 15,000 commercially available products from more than 1,900 manufacturers. Each listing provides brand name, manufacturer, cost, description and available evaluation. Products listed are for use in all aspects of independent living, including personal care, transportation, communication, and recreation. Information specialists conduct literature searches for the public and provide bibliographies tailored to specific requests. Call NARIC for information and fee structure. Abeldata can also be accessed through BRS Information Technologies, a commercial database vendor.

Agebase
A National Clearinghouse of Service Programs for the Elderly
The Brookdale Foundation Group
126 East 56th Street
New York, NY 10022-3668
(212) 308-7355 or (813) 334-1911

A continually growing clearinghouse that receives input from an ongoing survey of direct service programs for the elderly. An Agebase search provides current addresses, phone numbers, contact people, and a detailed description of every program including date established, population served, and current activities. Agebase will supply, free of charge, information on the subjects requested. Agebase is for professionals researching program ideas and for networking.

Ageline
National Gerontology Resource Center
American Association of Retired Persons
601 E Street NW
Washington, DC 20049
(202) 434-2277

Ageline, a computerized bibliographic database, provides citations to journal articles, books, government documents, reports, and research projects dealing with middle age and aging. Topics covered include family relationships, economics, population studies, health care services, and psychological and sociological aspects of middle and older age. Ageline is also available through BRS Information Technologies, a commercial database vendor.

Insurance Counseling
National Committee to Preserve Social Security and Medicare
2000 K Street, NW
Suite 800
Washington, DC 20006
(202) 822-9459

> The computerized Medigap Check-Up program that was available from the United Seniors Health Cooperative has now been updated with information on the new ten standard Medigap policies (Plans A–J) and is now available at no charge to non-profit organizations involved in insurance counseling. The software program has been renamed *Insurance Counseling* and is being distributed with a user manual. For more information, contact Edward Brenner.
>
> The software does comparisons of the policies based on information supplied by the policy holder, such as the premium cost by age, and then develops a grid for immediate comparison.

Vestbib
Vestibular Disorders Association (VEDA)
1015 NW 22nd Avenue
Portland, OR 97210-3709
(503) 229-7705

> Vestbib is a computerized bibliography of articles about dizziness, vertigo, and other inner ear balance problems. Sources are materials published in medical journals in English from 1988 on, with each entry including complete bibliographic information and citations of similar articles for additional sources. Most entries have an abstract of 50 to 300 words. VEDA can conduct custom searches on any topic related to vestibular disorders. There is a modest fee for this service.

Glossary

Accessory apartment   A separate, self-contained living unit created within an existing single-family home or attached to it. Also known as an in-law apartment, mother-in-law apartment, or granny flat. See also Echo Housing.

Activities coordinator   A person who develops, organizes, and directs programs that provide recreational, social, educational, and entertainment activities for residents of a nursing home, adult day-care facility, personal care home, or senior center.

Activities of daily living (ADLs)   Eating, dressing, bathing, toileting, using the telephone, taking medications, and other personal care activities.

Acute illness   A sudden illness such as a heart attack or stroke that develops rapidly with pronounced symptoms. The illness can be of short duration such as influenza.

Adaptive devices   Specialized products, hardware, and clothing that help people compensate for their disabilities and live, cope, and function more independently.

Adult day care   A day-care center with daily, weekly, or part-time schedules, offering health-related and rehabilitative services, social involvement, and activities to meet the needs of physically or mentally impaired elderly people. Also referred to as adult or geriatric care, therapeutic day care, day health care, or day hospital care.

Adult home   A facility designed for people who need personal attention with activities of daily living (see ADLs) but who maintain a

229

more independent life-style than that in a nursing home or personal care home. Usually does not include any level of nursing care. See also Assisted Living Facilities, Group Home.

Advance Medical Directive   A legal document produced by a competent person and addressed to the person's physician, or that appoints a legally designated health agent to make health care decisions. Also called advance medical instruction. Similar legal documents are health care proxy and medical power of attorney. See also Living Wills, Durable Power of Attorney, and Durable Power of Attorney for Health Care.

Aging in place   A phrase to describe a person's desire to continue living in his or her own home.

Aging network   Support and informational services available for older people within their local communities. This term also applies to the same services at the state and federal levels.

Allied health professionals   People with specialized training in a field related to medicine who work in collaboration with physicians or other health professionals.

Alzheimer's disease   A form of dementia that causes severe intellectual deterioration. It is a progressive, degenerative disease and is currently considered irreversible.

Aphasia   Loss of the ability to use or understand language.

Area Agency on Aging (AAA or Triple A)   Known also as a county office on aging. Usually a nonprofit agency or unit of local government with the responsibility for planning and coordinating services for people over age 60 in a designated geographical area.

Assisted living facilities   Residential facilities for those who need help with activities of daily living (see ADLs) within an environment that retains as high a level of independence as possible. May also be called adult homes, board-and-care homes, domiciliary care facilities, independent senior apartments, personal care homes, and residential care facilities.

Assistive devices   See Adaptive Devices.

Board-and-care homes   See Assisted Living Facilities.

Caregiver   A person who helps an elderly person with the activities of everyday living, medical care, or financial matters, or provides guidance, companionship, or interest, or provides more than one aspect of care. See also Long-Distance Caregiver and Primary Caregiver.

Caregiver support group   Groups led by a professional or a caregiver that allow caregivers to meet in a supportive, nonjudgmental atmosphere to express their feelings, share coping skills, and learn about resources, caregiver issues, and community services.

Care (case) management   Assessment, coordination, and monitoring of services provided directly to an elderly person. Care managers are trained professionals. Other terms for this service are geriatric care (case) managers, private geriatric care managers, or case workers. Some communities may provide case or care management free of charge through local nonprofit agencies. Most care management services are for-profit providers.

Care recipient or care receiver   An older person who requires some level of care and help from another person such as a relative, friend, health professional, or home-health aide.

Carrier watch   A U.S. Post Office program in which postal clerks and mail carriers watch for regular mail pickup by elderly residents who are registered with their post office. If mail is not picked up or taken in, an emergency contact is made. Not available in all communities.

Chore service   Help with repairs and chores inside and outside of a house or apartment, provided through the local Area Agency on Aging, volunteer programs, or youth groups to help older people live safely and comfortably in their own homes.

Chronic illness   A physical or mental disability that continues over a long period of time or recurs frequently. Chronic conditions often begin inconspicuously and the symptoms are less pronounced than in an acute illness. See also Acute Illness.

Companion   A person who helps an elderly individual with daily living activities only. A companion has no nursing responsibilities.

Congregate housing   Individual rental units, usually apartments, in a multiunit building or garden complex, planned and designed for the elderly. Supportive services such as meals, transportation, housekeeping, and social and recreational activities are usually available. See also Assisted Living Facilities.

Continuing care retirement community (CCCR)   Also known as a CCC, a continuing care community, or a life-care community. Most require an entrance fee plus a monthly maintenance fee. They offer a range of services and living arrangements from completely independent units (apartments) to assisted living arrangements (personal care) to intermediate and skilled nursing care (nursing home).

Custodial care   Help and supervision with ADLs such as dressing, eating, personal hygiene, and similar functions.

Dementia   A clinical term used to describe a group of brain disorders that disrupt and impair cognitive functions (thinking, memory, judgment, mood, personality, and social functioning). Dementia is not considered a part of the normal aging process.

Dependent care tax credit   Deductible tax credits for some home-care services and adult day-care services. Check with your local IRS office for new regulations on deducting payments to care for a dependent or disabled spouse in order to enable the caregiver to work or look for a job.

Diagnostic related groups (DRGs)   A method of grouping illnesses that is used to calculate Medicare Part A reimbursements to hospitals. DRGs are based on the patient's diagnosis rather than on the length of the hospital stay, and they may not equal the cost of treatment or the cost billed to the patient.

Discharge planner   A member of the professional staff of a hospital or nursing home who develops a plan for the future care of a patient prior to discharge. See also Social Worker.

Disposable medical equipment   Medical equipment that cannot be re-used and is disposed of immediately after use, such as adult diapers, feeding tubes, and hypodermic needles.

Domiciliary home care   A living arrangement for ambulatory and independent adults who require minimum supervision. See also Personal Care Home and Foster Care.

Durable medical equipment   Equipment that can be used repeatedly and is appropriate for home use. Such equipment includes hospital beds, wheelchairs, oxygen machines, and dialysis equipment.

Durable Power of Attorney   A power of attorney that stays in effect and is enforceable even if the principal becomes disabled or incapacitated. See also Advance Medical Directive, Living Will, and Power of Attorney.

Durable Power of Attorney for Health Care   Similar to a Durable Power of Attorney, a legal document that names an agent who will make health care decisions for the principal if that individual becomes unable to express wishes for himself or herself.

Echo housing   A self-contained, independent dwelling unit intended for older people and usually placed relatively near the home of adult children. Also known as a granny flat or elder cottage. See also Accessory Apartment.

Elder abuse   A general term for the mistreatment of the elderly, which may include physical, psychological, or sexual abuse; financial exploitation; or abandonment or neglect by a caregiver. Abuse may be committed by a family caregiver, other family members, hired or volunteer aides, or companions, and it may occur in either a home or an institutional setting.

Elder cottage   See Echo Housing.

Elder law or elder law attorney   The specific laws and legal specialty that deals with the rights and issues of the health, finances, and well-being of the elderly and the powers of other individuals and the state to control and interfere.

Emergency response systems   See Personal Emergency Response Systems (PERS).

Energy assistance   Assistance programs available in many states to help with home-energy problems for low-income persons. May be available even if heat and utilities are included in the rent.

Extended care facility   See Nursing Home.

Foster care   The placement of older people in need of minimum assistance into a family environment in a state-licensed foster home.

Friendly visitor   Also known as a senior companion. This person visits an elderly person at scheduled times to provide companionship and socialization.

Geriatric assessment   An evaluation of an older person's physical, psychological, and social condition by a professional team of specialists in geriatrics and gerontology, who make recommendations to the older person, family, and primary care doctor. Geriatric assessments are available in geriatric evaluation centers and are generally associated with hospitals.

Geriatric evaluation center   See Geriatric Assessment.

Geriatric medicine   The branch of medicine dealing with the disorders and conditions associated with the aging process. Also known as geriatrics.

Geriatrician   A physician who specializes in geriatric medicine.

Gerontologist   A psychologist who specializes in the mental and behavioral characteristics of the aging.

Group home   May be similar to an adult home, with unrelated residents living together. In a group home the residents may share in daily living activities. See also Shared Housing.

Guardianship   Powers granted by the court to a responsible adult, known as the guardian, to handle the affairs of another person who has been deemed incompetent or incapable of managing his or her own affairs and making rational decisions.

Health Care Power of Attorney   A legal agreement authorizing a person to act as the agent or attorney of another person to make health care decisions when that person becomes unable to do so for himself or herself. See also Advance Medical Directive.

Health maintenance organization (HMO)   A system in which medical services are provided at a selected and limited number of hospitals and doctors' offices for a fixed monthly fee and sometimes a copayment. Some HMOs are under contract to provide services to Medicare participants.

Home-delivered meals   See Meals-on-Wheels.

Home-health agency   A public or private organization with a staff of skilled nurses, homemakers, aides, and therapists to provide nursing, rehabilitative, and homemaking services to homebound patients with chronic or temporarily debilitating conditions and to individuals recovering in their own homes from major medical treatment.

Home-health aide   A trained medical assistant who works under the supervision of a nurse or physician and provides personal care services such as bathing and dressing, and health care procedures that do not require professional nursing skill.

Home-health care   Services such as bathing and dressing, preparing meals, administering medicines, and recording vital signs, which can be provided in a patient's home.

Home-health nurse   A professional nurse who makes home visits with orders from a doctor to evaluate the patient's condition and provide professional nursing care. Patients or family members may also be trained in home-health care.

Homemaker   A specially trained individual who provides household cleaning, cooking, grocery shopping, laundry, escort, and personal care for an elderly person. No nursing care is provided.

Home-matching program   See Shared Housing.

Hospice   Usually a combination of at-home and hospital care for terminally ill patients that combines medical and social services and is designed to help the patient and the family. Hospices emphasize pain control, symptom management, and emotional support rather than life-sustaining technology.

Incontinence   The loss of voluntary control over bladder or bowel functions.

Independent senior apartments   See Assisted Living Facilities.

Instrumental activities of daily living (IADLs)   Home-managed activities such as preparing meals, shopping, managing money, using the telephone, and doing light housework.

Intake worker   Usually the first person spoken to at a social service agency. The intake worker reviews the consumer's request and makes referrals to the proper department or service.

Intermediate care facility (ICF)   A nursing facility that provides help with personal or social care and a minimum of medical supervision.

Intestate   The condition of dying without a will.

Life-care community   See Continuing Care Retirement Community.

Living trust   An agreement between one individual and another individual or entity to manage and distribute the individual's property and assets.

Living Will   A legal document produced by a competent individual conveying his or her wishes regarding medical treatment for a life-threatening illness or injury if he or she becomes incompetent or unable to express these wishes. See also Advance Medical Directive, Durable Power of Attorney for Health Care.

Long-distance caregiver   Caregivers who provide care for an elderly person who lives some distance away from the caregiver.

Long-term care   A catchall phrase that describes a range of medical, nursing, social, and community services designed to help people with chronic health impairments or forms of dementia.

Long-term care insurance   Insurance policies issued by private companies designed to defray the costs of long-term care in nursing facilities as well as home-care services.

Meals-on-Wheels   Nutritionally balanced meals delivered on a regular basis to housebound elderly people for little or no cost.

Medicaid   A health care and health insurance program jointly financed by the federal and state governments for low-income people 65 and older as well as for disabled and low-income individuals.

Medicare   A federal health insurance program for people 65 and older and some disabled Americans, which helps defray many medical expenses.

Medicare assignment   An agreement whereby a doctor or other provider of medical care agrees to accept Medicare's payment schedule as payment in full, except for specific coinsurance and deductible amounts for which the patient is responsible.

Medigap insurance   Private health insurance policies intended to cover medical costs not fully covered or paid by Medicare. Also known as Supplemental Insurance.

Nursing home   A nursing facility that provides a full range of board, care, and medical services to those recovering from hospitalization or suffering from chronic illness, dementia, or other factors that make it impossible for them to live at home. See also Intermediate Care Facility and Skilled Nursing Care.

Occupational therapist (OT)   A licensed professional therapist who helps a person relearn activities of daily living through methods of rehabilitation and the use of adaptations and devices for the home environment to help the person function more independently.

Ombudsman services   Programs that advocate and protect the rights of residents in long-term care facilities by investigating complaints, mediating and resolving disputes, and initiating corrective actions.

Personal care home   See Assisted Living Facilities.

Personal emergency response system (PERS)   Equipment that monitors the safety of older people in their homes through signals electronically transmitted over the telephone and received at an emergency monitoring center.

Pharmaceutical assistance program   A state-run prescription copayment program for residents 65 years or older whose total annual income meets the state's participation requirements.

Physical therapist (PT)   A licensed professional therapist who treats impaired motion or disease through exercise, massage, hydrotherapy, or mechanical devices to improve physical mobility.

Power of attorney   A legal document in which an individual gives another person the authority to act on his or her behalf. See also Durable Power of Attorney.

Primary caregiver   A caregiver who has the main responsibility for helping and caring for an older person. The primary caregiver usually is the one who has the responsibility of making decisions and organizing care and services. See also Caregiver.

Primary care physician   The doctor a person calls on and sees first when a health problem occurs and on whom the patient relies for advice, referrals, and ongoing care.

Protective services   Services that support an adult who may be abused, neglected, or exploited. Available from social service agencies and state agencies. See also Elder Abuse.

Rehabilitative aids   See Adaptive Devices.

Representative payee   A person, public or nonprofit agency, or an institution that has been legally designated to receive the Social Security benefits intended for another and is legally required to use the money for the well-being of the original beneficiary.

Respite care   A service that provides primary caregivers with short-term relief from caregiving responsibilities. Respite care may be given in or out of the home.

Respite worker   A volunteer or paid worker who offers respite to primary caregivers in the caregiver's home, the respite worker's home, or an institutional setting.

Retirement community   Housing specifically designed for older adults, with recreational and social facilities. May also be called senior communities.

Sandwich generation   A popular phrase to describe people (primarily women) who have become the primary caregivers for parents or other elderly relatives and are sandwiched between the caregiving responsibilities for the elderly and for their own children.

Senility   See Dementia.

Senior centers   Neighborhood centers that offer a range of services, programs, and social, health, nutritional, educational, and recreational activities. Some are called clubs. Senior centers are for the well elderly.

Shared housing   A program available in some communities matching older individuals to live together in one house. One of the individuals may be the owner of the house. See also Group Housing.

Skilled nursing care   Supervision and medical treatment given by a registered nurse under the direction of a doctor 24 hours a day.

Skilled nursing facility (SNF)   A facility that provides 24-hour-a-day medical services by registered nurses, licensed practical nurses, or nurse aides for seriously ill or severely disturbed people who do not require hospitalization.

Social worker   A trained professional and licensed counselor who assists the elderly and their families in understanding and coping with the social, emotional, and psychological aspects of aging. The social worker coordinates, directs, and instructs in the accessing of services.

Supplemental insurance   See Medigap Insurance.

Supplemental Security Income (SSI)   A federal program of cash assistance to people with limited income and resources who are aged 65 or over, blind, or disabled.

Support group   See Caregiver Support Group.

Telephone reassurance program   A program in which frail, ill, or housebound people are called on a regular basis to check on their safety and to provide them with a personal contact.

Visiting nurse   A trained professional nurse who visits patients in their homes to monitor vital signs and physical condition, and carry out the physician's treatment orders.

Waiver of Premiums   A part of some long-term health care policies (usually considered for nursing home stays) where the insured, after receiving benefits for a number of days, pays no more premiums and continues to collect the benefits while becoming well. The policy holder pays nothing back and nothing is deducted from the policy holder's benefits. Once well (or discharged from a nursing home) the premiums resume.

Index